The Beauty of R.A.M.

Deepening Human Connections through Relationships, Accountability and Mentoring

By

Aaron L. Horn

The Beauty of R.A.M.

Front Cover Artwork

Mrs. Selma Schlesinger Cooper

TABLE OF CONTENTS

ACKNOWLEDGMENTS

Thank you God for giving me the gift of presenting my thoughts in the written word. You have blessed me beyond my wishes!

To my immediate family (Mom, Marc, Rita and Colette) thank you for your persistent support and encouragement.

To mom, thank you for being my editor, critic and staunch supporter. You are the best mom ever!

To grandma, I feel your spirit and protection every day from heaven. Thank you for protecting me with your spiritual guidance.

To the love of my life and Black Queen, Colette AnnMarie Reid, thank you for demonstrating enduring love to me every day.

To the Horn, Jackson, Reid, Reynolds, Moore, Parish, Threadgill, Gillette, Midget, Kimble, Austin, Marshall, Arnold, and other families, thank you for unrelenting love and support.

To all of my aunts, uncles, and cousins (Jan, Paulette, Lise, Jeannie, Katherine, Archie Jr., Lucias, Danny, Craig, Donnell, Demetrius, Chris Moore, Chris Horn, Big Victor, Lil Victor, Bridgette, April, Tamiaka, Janetta, Amanda, Kevin, Jerome and others). Thank you for your love and support!

To my extended family, Auntie Robey, Uncle Eddie, Auntie Marilyn, Auntie Kim Stepney, Auntie Linda Midget, Cousin Kim Kimble, Auntie Robbie Austin, Auntie Marie Marshall, Auntie Maxine Arnold, Cousin Eric and Gwen, Cousin Tamar, Cousin Joanna, Cousin Rebecca, Cousin Jonathan, Cousin Abraham, Uncle Rosco Westbrook, Auntie Connie, Uncle Flash, Auntie Tammie, Uncle and Auntie Loyal Moore, Cousin Sabrina Reynolds, Cousin Clarissa Ringer, and Uncle Billie and Auntie Mikelyn Threadgill (Rest in Peace). Thank you for instrumental support!

To my God family, Pat, Brenda, Zachery, Ronnette, Will, Ria, and Ruby. Thank you for always supporting my efforts. Love you all!

FOREWORD

As a native San Franciscan and long-term friend and colleague of Dr. Aaron L. Horn for more than 20 years, I feel honored to express my appreciation regarding this most profound prose on Relationship, Accountability and Mentoring (R.A.M.). At my core, I am a husband to a beautiful wife of 18 years, a father of two young African American men and a senior manager, nearly three decades, for a Fortune 100 company.

I first began working with Dr. Horn several years ago, seeking his guidance on further enhancing my personal and professional endeavors. As my executive coach and mentor, Dr. Horn consulted with me and immediately leveraged his R.A.M. approach. The results dramatically shifted my perception of self, which consequently significantly improved my ability to effectively engage with colleagues, family and others. Through Dr. Horn's R.A.M. coaching, specifically the implementation of his Horn Accountability Instrument (H.A.I.), I was able to learn how to effectively attune with others, for more productive and sustained relationships.

Today, my ability to relate with others (i.e., emotional mindfulness) in a variety of dynamic personal and professional capacities, is light years beyond my baseline. As a result of Dr. Horn's tailored approach to improving human connection, I am better equipped to develop and implement precise plans that address those I engage with using comprehensive solutions that meet people where they are and address their specific needs. In yet another detailed manuscript on his proficiency in relationships, Dr. Horn vividly captures his R.A.M. process in a way that inspires, motivates and encourages us all to be thoughtful and productive people of integrity.

Mr. Robert Lucas

Robert Lucas is a senior manager for a Fortune 100 company. He has held positions in Sales, Marketing, Solutions Consulting and Industrial Engineering servicing various businesses in the San Francisco and Greater Bay Area region for over 25 years.

PREFACE

I am interested in promoting my technique of human engagement, otherwise known as R.A.M. (Relationship, Accountability and Mentoring), to help individuals in all professions enhance their ability to relate with other human beings. My style of relating with human beings, developed over the course of my lifetime, has been used with almost everyone in nearly every field, primarily with colleagues and clients in the field of human service (i.e., teaching, counseling and coaching). In particular, I have used R.A.M. as a means to improve containment procedures of young Black males. By containment procedures, I mean "the keeping of Black Males" in schools as opposed to removal procedures – "the suspending and expulsion of Black Males."

For this reason, I want to share my experience and passion with the reader about enhancing ways of relating with human beings, especially young Black males. Overall, what I found as a teacher, counselor and coach, working with young Black males in multiple capacities, is that if you take the time to relate with young Black Males, they are more willing to minimize their involvement in high risk behaviors and improve academically (Horn, 2010, 2012).

Therefore, it is my wish to improve how we as human beings relate with one another, particularly young Black males, in order to "loosen up the restraints" that have many young Black males in an ever-present state of anxiety. Most often, I use my method of R.A.M. with young Black males either in a group or one-on-one session, resulting in a significantly positive impact on their overall academic interest and development. Hence, my desire is that after reading and understanding my examples of R.A.M. in the subsequent chapters, readers will be able to enhance their own practice of relationship techniques with the people they encounter, especially high-risk Black males.

CHAPTER 1

THE GENEALOGY OF R.A.M.

For the reader to comprehend the complexity of R.A.M., I will describe its origination. In this chapter, I describe the key ingredients that helped to foster and cultivate my concept of R.A.M. (Relationships, Accountability and Mentoring). All of these ingredients (i.e., lived experiences) comingled to produce a process that has allowed me to deepen my connection with human beings. As a result, I assert that R.A.M. can be added to the research on human relations as one system for deepening human connection.

The Resiliency of Momma and Grandma

The concept of developing intimate relationships between human beings, the first element of R.A.M., was first developed in me as a young child, as early as I can remember. In fact, the resiliency of my grandmother (Cora Lee Reynolds) and my mother (Ursulanda Horn) literally gave birth to my idea of R.A.M. Before my view of R.A.M. was born, my mom was giving birth to me on December 2, 1969, at 2:26am at General Hospital in San Francisco, California. After my birth, we briefly lived in the Hunters Point neighborhood, eventually moving to Daly City, California. While growing up in Daly City, I remember meeting friends rather quickly as a child. I was a gregarious, adventurous young man with a taste for nature—I loved playing in the hills of our new residential neighborhood.

On many occasions, I remember meeting friends at my elementary school (Daniel Webster) through my usual elated introductory response which sounded something like, "Hi…. my name is Aaron." Along with my radiant gap-toothed smile, I always had a way of capturing the hearts and souls of other human beings. Hence, at an early age, I practiced the art of deepening connections with human beings. As I grew into a young adult, I enthusiastically and wholeheartedly introduced myself to everyone as if they were the most important person in the world—something that just came naturally to me. Being open and present to others is the first step in building an enduring and meaningful relationship.

Moreover, accountability, the second aspect of R.A.M., was cultivated in me through my mother Ursula Horn and Grandmother Cora Lee Reynolds. As a child, I realized that my mother had a profound way of communicating with everyone. She is a fierce communicator. Often loud and firm, yet always commanding the space she inhabits. In this regard, my mother embodies R.A.M. As a case in point, I remember when my brother and I were children; we would sometimes act out in public. Reminiscing, I was able to observe and learn how my mother utilized R.A.M. to reprimand us. After issuing her one and only verbal warning, my mother would begin admonishing us briefly without shame. In this way, I observed my mother holding us accountable through her direct yet cautious way of accountability engagement.

My late grandmother was another accountability mentor who laid the foundation for my ability to hold myself and others accountable. She had an unfathomable way of holding human beings accountable. One of the most memorable accountability moments in my life occurred when I was a teenager. I remember my grandma putting my "butt in check," as some of us say in the Black community. I had arrogantly walked into her home with my Jerry Curl (a processed method of maintaining one's hair) dripping with oil off my neck and onto her linoleum floor. As my grandmother cautiously rolled her eyes at me and rebuked me in her usual staunch voice, "...boy... you betta go wipe that stuff off your neck....your head is dripping wet Aaron..." (Researcher Journal, 2015).

Although I was slightly embarrassed at my grandma's reproach, I hastily ran into the bathroom and wiped my neck, which was full of grease and guck. In this manner, my grandmother did not care about the newly invented way that many Black Americans used to process their hair. No, my grandmother cared only about her grandson representing our race (Black Americans) in the utmost respectful way. In essence, the wiping of grease from my neck represented not only respect for my grandmother but for the entire race of Black Americans.

Through her firm reproof, I learned that holding people accountable involved respect for self and culture.

Even more, my mother and grandmother have always been my mentors, the third part of R.A.M., while I was growing up. I have always believed that mentoring involves the shadowing of a more experienced individual over another less experienced individual in order to share and transfer behaviors, values, and skills. By this means, my grandmother and mother mentored the spirit of resiliency for me. As a single parent, my mother exemplified the essence of a mentor every day of her life. For example, after my mom and dad divorced, I watched my mom provide a stable household throughout my entire child and adolescent years. My mother worked every day to pay the rent on our home and provide food for my brother and me without ever breaking down in front of us. In this way, I looked up to my mother as a mentor because of her ability to maintain a household through her resiliency.

As she modeled the role of a mentor, my mother demonstrated to me daily the Seven Principles of Kwanza (otherwise known as the Nguzo Saba). These distinct principles include: 1) Umoja (unity), 2) Kujichagulia (self-determination), 3) Ujima (collective work and responsibility), 4) Ujamaa (cooperative economics), 5) Nia (purpose), 6) Kuumba (creativity) and 7) Imani (faith) (Wilson, 1991).

On most occasions, my mother demonstrated Imani (faith). While watching my mother awake every day to attend work as a House Parent for the San Francisco Unified School District, I was astonished at her faith. In many of her conversations with our relatives, my mother would always include that she prayed everyday as she raised my brother and me. Even more, I would watch my mother get on her knees and pray, instilling a reverence for faith at an early age. As I grew into young adulthood, I found myself getting on my knees praying for God to help me. Thereby, I have benefited from my mother's modeling of Imani by including prayer in my everyday life.

Similarly, my grandmother mentored her spirit of resilience to me throughout my life. Although she passed away four years ago, I can feel her spirit of resilience residing within me. My grandmother was born and raised in New Orleans, Louisiana, and eventually made her way to San Francisco, California, to follow the shared dreams of a better life with my grandfather, Archie Reynolds. After settling here in the mid-1950's, my grandmother obtained a series of working class jobs, including helping my grandfather become one of San Francisco's leading entrepreneurs. While supporting a family of six children, and other extended family members, my grandmother maintained a stable household by cleaning, cooking and working continuously without grievance—just like my mother. For these reasons, I respect my grandmother as a mentor because she also demonstrated resiliency.

As Wilson (1991) describes, my grandmother mentored her spirit of Umoja (unity) to me while I was growing up. When I was young, my grandmother always taught me about the significance of keeping the family together, especially through family dinners and gatherings. When I grew up, my grandmother further sustained Umoja through her constant gatherings of holiday birthdays, dinners and anniversaries of various family members. This spirit of Umoja still impacts me today as a middle-aged adult. For example, my cousin Demetrius recently celebrated a birthday. Because I was inundated with employment responsibilities and previous commitments, I thought I was not going to attend his birthday celebration in Oakland. Yet, to my disbelief, I was able to coordinate my schedule to arrive before the end of his birthday celebration. The moral of the story is that even though I have become busy with my life, I try to attend all of my family celebrations because of my grandmother's mentoring of Umoja.

Finally, both my grandmother and mother taught me how to deeply connect with human beings. For instance, my mother is the connection expert. I always say that if the Board of Behavioral Science (BBS) began issuing honorary therapist licenses to individuals who demonstrated years of unyielding engagement to connect with other human beings, similar to the process of forming meaningful relationships in therapy, I would nominate my mother as the shining example of an effective therapist. My mother exemplifies every sense of human connections. As long as I can remember, my mother had a unique way of connecting with human beings that she modeled to me every day.

When I was a child, I watched my mother engage with family members, friends and colleagues to the point where people sought her out for individual counseling. I spent countless hours *ear hustling* my mother's phone conversations as she intensely and passionately answered the repetitive questions from her emotionally distraught friends, often resulting in significant, positive life-changes. In this way, my mother is a natural-born therapist. In fact, she always had a way of making you feel so comfortable that you want to tell her your whole life story in one face-to-face, sit-down session.

What makes my mother's human connection skill so unique is that she actively listens to the other person uninterruptedly. I still find this ability to be rare in today's generation of wanting answers now (i.e., the microwave generation). My mother's attentive listening of R.A.M. has helped me navigate many disconcerting life obstacles. One particular deep-connecting session occurred between my mother and me decades ago when I was in my early twenties.   I remember struggling with dating, like so many young adults, feeling ashamed and malcontent with my past relationship choices. As I sat in the living room pondering random thoughts of unsuccessful dating, I opened up to my mom who noticed my obvious unhappiness. After listening to me uninterruptedly for at least an hour, she spoke in a soft voice, uttering the most memorable words to me ever, "I notice you tend to behave like a social worker in your relationships" (Researcher Journal, 2015).

Ouch! These words of absolute truth would stay with me for the rest of my life. Through her steadfast listening, my mother unabashedly offered me advice that was spot on truthful. My mother elaborated saying that I tended to always find women who were "needy" and "disadvantaged." This then allows me to fill a void in their lives by becoming the "savior" that I think they need, allowing for a vicious cycle of co-dependence. My mother warned me about my attraction to needy women because this would set me up for failure later on in life—always trying to be the helper in a relationship. I accepted her advice wholeheartedly and thus deepened my relationship with my mother because of her ability to listen attentively and name my stuff (ineffective dating skills) without making me feel ashamed. Now that I am in a healthy relationship with the love of my life,

Colette Reid, I appreciate how my mother's ability to connect with me empowered me to make better decisions regarding healthy relationships—choosing a very healthy life partner in Colette.

Therefore, R.A.M. was birthed in me through my heritage of family. For these reasons, R.A.M. was inspired by my strong mother and grandmother who spent their life (1) authentically relating with me during our time spent together, (2) holding me accountable with their strong sense of self and (3) mentoring strength and resiliency as they unassumingly supported their households.

Big Brother Eli

The foundation of R.A.M. would not be completely understood if I failed to mention the significant impact of my older brother Eli (aka Big Brother). My big brother Eli has always mentored me through his life skills teaching. My brother is a tall and handsome man with a humble presence. Standing around six feet four inches, he has a powerful and gentle way of teaching life skills. As early as I can recall, my brother taught me how to navigate life as a Black man in mainstream America.

On several occasions, my brother reinforced the meaning of being organized and always prepared for potential employment. For instance, I remember when I first began developing my employment skills as a young adult. Due to my lack of workforce experience, my brother persistently reminded me to always update my resume so that I captured my skills and abilities in a timely and organized manner. Hence, my brother believed in the prompt updating of resumes, especially those of young Black males, so that "we can be prepared for" the unexpected future opportunities. As a result of his life skills mentoring, I am now updating my 20-page curriculum vitae (an extended professional resume) so that it accurately portrays my proficiencies gained over 20 years of teaching, counseling and coaching.

I have also benefited from my big brother's mentoring of resiliency. Growing up as a child, I timidly observed my brother working various jobs successfully. Most of my brother's success at employment, similar to his success today, is due to his ability to use

R.A.M. to deepen his connections with other human beings. Case in point, I remember my brother working for this racist employer who owned a car wash. My brother would avoid most of this Caucasian American's microaggressions by focusing on his work and evading the racist dialogue that my brother witnessed on a daily basis. In so doing, my brother used accountability (i.e., the focusing on his job) to navigate any involvement with this employer's banter. Thereby, after watching my big brother navigate some of the most insidious forms of institutional racism, I have learned to use R.A.M. in a similar strategic way to encounter institutional racism.

Recently, as one of the few Black male counseling psychology graduate students in my program, I encountered daily institutional racism. As a Black graduate student using R.A.M. effectively, I was able to reconnect with my Black community and became more aware of my Afrocentric culture by attending church, more family gatherings and staying connected with my passion for helping Black males achieve. Furthermore, as a Black graduate student using R.A.M. to survive, I became more comfortable with my own style of participation in this class, given the majority of white students and the feeling of being outnumbered.

In addition, as a Black graduate student I survived by using R.A.M. because I was extremely supportive to my peers. During my tenure as a graduate student, I listened to many of my peers' frustrations with their personal lives and their struggles with academia, participating in out-of-class, critical consciousness-raising dialogues. Many of these pseudo-counseling relationships involved my white peers who had been open and honest with me and reached out to me in various ways for support. Thereby, I was able to minimize my judgmental beliefs about my white peers through my R.A.M. spirit.

Lastly, as a Black graduate student, I used R.A.M. efficiently and successfully to buffer my encounters with microaggressions in my program. Sue et al. (2007) define racial microaggressions as

> brief and commonplace daily verbal, behavioral, or environmental indignities, whether intentional or unintentional, that communicate hostile, derogatory, or negative racial slights and insults toward people of color. Perpetrators of

microaggressions are often unaware that they engage in such communications when they interact with racial/ethnic minorities. (p. 271)

Although some of these microaggressions triggered me to suppress my emotions, I used R.A.M. to talk with friends and colleagues through open-ended dialogues. As a result of observing my big brother's use of R.A.M. to successfully navigate institutional racism, I also used R.A.M. to rid myself of any malcontent feelings as a Black graduate student. In so doing, I learned, by observing my brother's use of R.A.M., to foster authentic caring relationships with every human being. As a result, I was able to graduate with two prestigious graduate degrees from a University with a predominant Caucasian American graduate student body.

Rites of Passage

In traditional Africa, rites of passage were a means to strip down the young village boys of their old way of life in order to prepare them for a new way of living. Wilson (1991) expounds on rites of passage as, "…these rites may symbolize and certify the completion of certain special training and preparation to undertake a new social role and function…" (p.48). Similarly, my particular rites of passage included (1) playing junior college football, (2) pledging a prominent Black Fraternity and (3) completing a five-year contract as an elite military paratrooper. These rites of passage events in totality helped to solidify my R.A.M. foundation. Below, I explain each rite of passage experience chronologically as they transpired in my life.

Home of the RAMS

It was the home of the RAMS, not R.A.M. but the RAMS. As a young, ambitious junior college football player, I became absorbed and immersed into the prestigious and infamous City College of San Francisco (CCSF) Ram football organization. My short-lived football career with the Rams would turn out to be one of the most memorable rites of passage experiences during my lifespan development. During the years of 1988-1989, the renowned CCSF RAM football team embedded the spirit of endurance within my well-developed cloak of R.A.M. If you had ever felt the cool crisp air blowing into your hair at a traditional San Francisco 49ers football or Giants game at Candlestick Park, then you have an idea of the cool breeze that would tickle your ear lobes at the home of the CCSF Ram football team during the autumn. Playing football for the CCSF Rams during the '88 and '89 seasons contributed to a prolific time in my life. My CCSF football experience cultivated endurance all throughout my bones.

It was a hot summer morning in 1989 when I first walked on the field of the CCSF Rams. Being raised in San Francisco, I always knew of or heard about the Rams football program. The Rams were known for having some of the most prestigious junior college football athletes that ever walked the fertile grounds of San Francisco, including O.J. Simpson himself (aka The Juice). Playing for the CCSF Rams promised to be a one-in-a-lifetime opportunity, which can lead to a potential four-year college football scholarship at the end of a two-year journey. The CCSF Rams had the most productive offense, defense and special teams in the country. Playing for the CCSF Rams was akin to playing for the 1980's 49er team because they were known for one thing only—winning. As I walked onto that hot, sultry field that summer day, I would be transformed by what was to follow—the CCSF Ram rites of passage.

During the following weeks, I was quickly introduced and transitioned into the Ram methodology—sound familiar? Not R.A.M. but RAM. This procedure included engaging in rigorous morning drills of running, hitting and learning the extensive offensive and defensive playbook schemes. After a short lunch at McDonald's or Beep's Burgers on Ocean Avenue, we returned for our afternoon practice where we repeated the same routine in addition to more cardiovascular drills. The Rams favorite drill was entitled "Georgia 20's." I actually don't know where the football team acquired this drill or the origin of the name, but the physical requirements were extreme to say the least. Each player, donned full football gear (i.e., helmet, shoulder pads, etc.) and engaged in 20 push-ups, followed by 20 sit-ups. Next, the players had to complete 19 push-ups followed by 19 sit-ups. This process was repeated until we all reached the number one. I can't begin to tell you how many push-ups and sit-ups we completed. Can you do the math?

What I did learn from the "Georgia 20" experience was endurance. After completing such a rigorous and repetitive exercise, I realized that our coaching staff was not only trying to build up physical stamina, they were instilling mental stamina as well. The Georgia 20 exercise would haunt me for the rest of my life because the endurance that I learned from completing those push-ups and sit-ups would resonate with me in the life circumstances that would soon occur to me as a young Black male in America. For instance, I remember playing against an all-white team located around the Sacramento, California, region. During the game, many of their white players chanted "Go home nigger" as we each laid punishing blows upon each other. As the game continued, I remember becoming fatigued due to the humid heat on that summer August afternoon at our home field.

As the game played on, I became increasingly fatigued yet motivated at the same time because of my physical, mental and spiritual fitness. My endurance kicked-in to full gear and I began playing like a lion in the jungle on the hunt for his kill. I was sweeping across the field, leaping in the air and jumping on the ball every chance I could get. I was a six foot two, 222-pound defensive end who was filled with quiet rage. My endurance from the Georgia 20's had fueled my passion and intensity so that I could play as aggressively and as focused as my defensive team needed me to be that day. Despite their racist antics of intimidation, our team beat the living day lights out of them, sending them home like wounded dogs with their tails between their legs. The endurance I learned at CCSF allowed me to play in this game with fierceness. The same aggressiveness I use to navigate my life today.

Last year, I began working with a nonprofit organization as a clinician. When I began my assignment, I was bombarded with unfinished paperwork and other projects from the previous clinician that needed immediate attention. As these assignments and their ascribed due dates began to overwhelm me, I reflected upon my "Georgia 20" days at CCSF. After one month, I completed five treatment plans, five assessments and over 200 pages of progress notes. Despite succumbing to walking pneumonia, I had reorganized all of my transferred clients' files so that the agency could recoup their delayed medical payments for these services. Although I received numerous honors and compliments for my restructuring efforts, I quietly knew where I had gathered the wherewithal to complete these well-overdue assignments. It was the rigorous endurance I had internalized when I was a young, fit defensive end playing for the legendary CCSF Rams.

The Pride of Alpha Phi Alpha

The second most proficient rite of passage experience was when I officially joined the most prestigious African American Fraternity in the world—Alpha Phi Alpha Fraternity Incorporated (AΦA). Being involved with AΦA meant pride in my African ancestry. African American fraternities and sororities have been an integral part of the African diaspora for many years. Joining the ranks of Alpha men meant that I was exposed to the most educated Black men on campus. My pride in being an Alpha man stemmed from my adoration of some of the most admired Black men in the United States, including W.E.B. DuBois and Martin Luther King, Jr. The history of Alpha Phi Alpha is filled with rich African ancestral pride.

Alpha Phi Alpha was the first inter-university Greek-letter community established for African Americans. Seven African American college men at Cornell University in Ithaca, New York, recognized the need for a resilient bond of comradeship among African descendants in this country and formed the fraternity. Like many Black organizations that occupied space at predominately white college campuses, AΦA's initial purpose was to promote the academic efforts of students of color, particularly underserved students. AΦA's founding principles included scholarship, fellowship, good character, and the uplifting of humanity. I pledged AΦA at San Francisco State University (SFSU) in December of 1992 and have never looked back. I am an Alpha man for life.

When I first began the process of becoming an AΦA at SFSU, I was a senior in college. Most young men in college who pledge fraternities experience binge drinking and naked pool diving. In the pledge process of AΦA, none of these childish pranks occurred. The pledge process of Alpha men involved rigorous academic testing, frequent volunteer experiences and countless interviews with AΦA officials to assess the goodness-of-fit (i.e., suitability) of individual pledges for becoming an Alpha man. As I achieved each step of becoming an Alpha man, my cultural pride increased with every task. I was completing the processes of becoming a member of the first inter-collegiate African American Greek Fraternity. Becoming an Alpha meant making my family increasingly proud of their grandson, nephew, cousin and son.

After receiving the news that I "crossed the burning sands" (i.e., official recognition of pledge completion at SFSU), I was gleefully excited. I remember coming home shouting aloud to my mother, "...I did it momma...I did it.... I am an Alpha... I am an Alpha..... A-Phi....A-Phi....A-Phi..." (Researcher Journal, 2015). My pledge process reinforced within me basic core human values such as humility, courage and pride in my African ancestry. Pride in being an educated Black man was what I took from this entire pledging process. Shortly after I became an Alpha man, I rededicated my life to serving my community by researching, reporting and discussing the most efficient ways to uplift underserved families. Since becoming an Alpha man, my cultural pride has allowed me to start my own consulting business, publish several books on young Black males and obtain several degrees that directly and indirectly help to better serve my community. AΦA rekindled cultural pride within me, which has, in turn, reignited my passion for helping underserved families, especially young Black males.

The Polishing Process of the Military

"I hear the chopper hovering...
(Chorus Responds: I hear the chopper hovering)
It hovers overhead...
(Chorus Responds: It hovers overhead)
The medic says he wounded...
(Chorus Responds: The medic says he wounded)
But I know he's dead...
(Chorus Responds: But I know he's dead)
Airborne, orne...orne...orne...
(Chorus Responds: Airborne, orne...orne..orne...)

Ranger…er…er…er…er…
(Chorus Responds: Ranger…er…er…er…er…)"

That inspirational song, which continues to be music to my ears today, is one of the United States Army's most dynamic marching songs. This song, sung during various marches on base and in the field, helped me to stay motivated because the Army served as the polishing process of R.A.M! As delineated above, R.A.M. was birthed in me through genetics—my mother, grandmother and brother's resiliency. However, the cultivation of R.A.M. occurred during the course of the most monumental portion of my lifespan development— my five years as a United States Soldier. After my mother, grandmother and brother laid a solid R.A.M. foundation, the military completed the final construction through their "R.A.M. polishing" process of making me into a solider.

What the military did for me and to me is often inexplicable in words. The United States Army was a place where I would come to develop a fond, loving relationship for accountability. As I began my transitional process into the military on that cool 1998 December morning in Fort Benning, Georgia (the base for new soldier basic military training), I immediately gained a deeper understanding of accountability. The military deemed this process as "becoming soldierized"—a process of breaking down a civilian and reconstructing him or her into a United States Military soldier.

As I reflect further on this December morning, I can visualize the delightful Drill Sergeants of Fort Benning using various descriptive words to transition us off from our first-class transportation services (emptied out of cattle trucks), into the processing center. They eloquently called for us to come into the transition center to be processed, "Get the (expletive) off the truck…now….move it….move it…move it…" (Researcher Journal, 2015). Yes, the sweet words of the U.S. Army Drill Sergeant! How these words saturated my soul over the next six months in basic training and advanced infantryman training (AIT). It was at this moment in time, approximately 1:00am in the morning that I came to understand and appreciate a new meaning of accountability. Henceforth, I learned the importance of the military's do-it-now/sense-of-urgency style of accountability.

Additionally, this do-it-now form of accountability was further emphasized by awakening the solider every day at 6:00am to prepare us for the day. As soldiers, we had to awake every day and dress in either our standard dress uniform or physical fitness attire. Regardless, both uniforms had to be properly organized, including "spit" shined boots, with shirts tucked in neatly with no dangling pieces of yarn or cloth. This process was accompanied by a loud trumpet echoing over the entire base playing a standard military musical chorus called reveille. The reveille-awakening morning routine was highly organized and mandatory. The army did not allow any soldier for any reason to miss reveille, unless they had prior approval or were severely ill. For me, reveille signified the beginning of a new day, a new journey and a new meaning to life. For the army, reveille was the commencement of the mission.

Thus, reveille enhanced my concept of R.A.M. in that the "awakening" of my spirit at 6:00am every day represented an awakening of R.A.M. After being exposed to this 6:00am code of daily emergence in the military, I incorporated this same principle in my life today, awakening everyday no later than 6:00am. In this way, the military's "wake up and do-it-now" accountability taught me the importance of starting my day with a do-it-now R.A.M. spirit. Furthermore, when I awakened every morning to reveille as a soldier in the military, our only focus was on the mission of the day.

Similarly, R.A.M. works best when I am focused on my mission of the day. In fact, I am focused at this very moment in my life right now. Over the past two weeks (July 1st – July 15th), I completed my final draft manuscript for this very book before submitting it to my editor. By this means, the purpose of my very existence for these two weeks was to complete this book and I did just that (i.e., "do-it-now" R.A.M.). This concept of completion was already developed within me from my mother, grandmother and brother but the military reasserted its purpose in my life through the concept of reveille—completing the mission of the day.

As I continued my service in the military, my theory of R.A.M. would become strengthened and further developed through the introduction of the notorious military road march. Road marches are a standard means of soldier-preparedness in the military. The general purpose of road marches is to help soldiers prepare for battle in various environments, including overcoming extreme temperatures and terrains. They usually range from 5 to 50 miles of distance, depending on the mood, the original declaration of the mission, and the commander in charge. Most of my road marches were an average of 50 miles long.

After five years of experiencing road marches, I fell in love with accountability again. The reason for my newfound appreciation of accountability existed because I found that road marches bred accountability within the soldier. For example, in order to prepare for a road march, a soldier must take careful consideration into each detail of accountability, including (1) water management, (2) equipment adjustment, and (3) gear coordination. These three distinct details of road marching responsibility can usually make or break some of the most elite soldiers. When one or more of these issues are not properly organized or coordinated, soldiers can become brutally injured.

Case in point, during one of my routine 50-mile road marches, a soldier in my battalion began weaving back and forth. Our battalion eventually assessed that this soldier was suffering from dehydration and fatigue. We had been road marching for at least 12 hours with minimal breaks. The army called this simulated battle preparation. As I was engagingly perusing my surroundings during the march (I loved to road march), this soldier plunged face first into the dirt. After our medical team attended to this soldier's basic needs, wiping clean the crusty scar tissue and mixtures of blood and dirt on his face, he was up on his feet in no time, continuing the long awaiting journey of our 50-mile road march. This soldier's infirmity taught me that preparation is essential to successful navigation through life. Spontaneously, I learned that preparation (i.e., R.A.M.-preparedness) can minimize calamity—both personal and professional.

After learning this concept of military R.A.M. readiness, I began applying its application to all of my personal and professional tasks, inevitably increasing my completion rate and efficiency of each organizational task. Most recently, I used my newly developed R.A.M. accountability to complete a succession of very important tasks including (1) coordinating my weekend schedule to attend family members' birthdays, friends' weddings and vacation travel for the year 2014-2015 with minimal financial conflict, (2) completed my case management paperwork which is due in a 24-hour turnaround for the past year every day without delay, (3) coordinated my personal and business schedule to complete my mandated jury duty service, (4) submitted deferment forms of my student loans in a timely manner, (5) coordinated my Board of Behavioral Science licensure paperwork for submission with appropriate timing, (6) managed my finances to attend to my numerous upcoming automobile repairs and (7) prepared my schedule to organize writing hours to finish this manuscript (Book #3) which is now complete.

To the lay person, the above-mentioned may not seem astounding but to a former Airborne Ranger who had to prepare for multiple deployments with hundreds of assigned daily tasks to complete, this above preparation is critical. As a result, the preparation that involved successful road marching preparation and awakening every day at 6:00am with precise military dress code for 5 years allowed me to further my principle of R.A.M. This includes, adding principles of do-it-now urgency with highly intensive preparation. In this way, road marching and awakening in the military allowed me to appreciate the significance of accountability.

The Importance of Silence

The final ingredient, if you will, of R.A.M. involves silence. Although academic research has shown the newly coined mental health term of "mindfulness" to yield healthy results in our brains and hearts, we all know that good ol' silence goes a long way. Magee (2015) stated "Research shows that mindfulness practices help us focus, give us greater control over our emotions, and increase our capacity to think clearly and act with purpose" (para. 5). On the other hand, as an academician and R.A.M. expert, I find that silence is the key ingredient of effective R.A.M. delivery because it replenishes my spirit. As I sit in silence now, overlooking the plush green grass that paints the vast mountain tops of Point Reyes, California, I reflect on how silence has helped me to practice R.A.M. successfully for 20 years.

For example, I can't remember the day when I finally began to use silence as my number one coping skill for navigating life successfully, but I do remember using it successfully when I faced potential life-altering obstacles. Silence has helped me to solve relationship issues, improve financial plans and reenergize myself. Silence has helped to protect my spirit of R.A.M. by allowing me to take care of me first. By starting and ending each day in silence, I have become a more effective practitioner of R.A.M.

For instance, one of the most powerful aspects of silence is that it allows you to "slow down." By slowing down, I found that I am able to coordinate my day and organize my personal and professional tasks. I call this the power of reflective R.A.M. By reflecting on my day, taking into account all of the designated steps, I make better decisions on how to prioritize and accomplish my tasks. Although this process is similar to the military preparation processes of R.A.M., it's not the same. In fact, preparing for and reflecting are similar yet different types of processes. For me, I found that preparation focuses on "doing of something" in the future and reflection involves "thinking about the doing of something" in retrospect.

Even more, reflection is everything. Without reflection, I find that I become discombobulated and confused. By all means, this reflective R.A.M. process allows me to become spiritually grounded, thinking about my day in its entirety, before I begin implementing R.A.M. This silencing and reflection process is unique in that it must not be taken lightly. Thus, reflection through silence helps me maintain the authenticity and delivery of R.A.M.

Sizing People Up

Sizing people up is one of the foremost concepts behind fostering authentic R.A.M. relationships. It is important to note that I do not want to confuse "sizing up" someone with a judgmental process. Instead, I use sizing people up as a means of observing people who are similar to me (i.e., people who demonstrate a spirit of R.A.M.). Therefore, I will describe how I acquired and use my techniques to size people up. These methods include observing and listening. These skills were developed over time by various people, organizations, and environmental factors. Most significantly, my mother helped me acquire these techniques by watching her model each one. Eventually, I internalized each technique and used them to size people up.

Observing.

Watching my mother observe her friends as I was growing up would in the long run help me observe (as a sizing up process) my friends later in life. For example, my mother would always watch people whom she befriended for years before proclaiming them as friends. This occurred for my mother's best friend, Connie, whom she has known over 40 years. When I asked about their relationship, my mother explained that Connie always interacted with our family positively.

As children, they met in junior high school and became friends. My mother explained that Connie (aka Auntie Connie) remained the same caring and dependable friend from their childhood. My mother articulated Auntie Connie's friendship as, "Connie was always there for me....when I needed her...she was always there..." (Researcher Journal, 2015). One particular example occurred when my mother and father divorced. Many people were trying to inform my mother about "how to divorce" my dad. On the other hand, Auntie Connie stood by silently in support of my mother without making any suggestions. As my mother put it, "she just knew how to be there for me..." By this means, my mother has been able to observe Auntie Connie's unwavering friendship through her positive interactions with our family—verifying her as a stable and trustworthy friend.

In the same way, I observe people in reference to my mother's friendship with Auntie Connie. For instance, I have known one of my best friends, Delmar Johnson (aka DJ), for 20 years. We both attended CCSF where we played football. I actually knew about Delmar in high school because we played for opposing teams. During one of our high school football games, he literally snapped (fractured) the hip bone of one of our star running backs. Now that was power! Delmar is a short, muscular Black male, who stands all of five feet six inches tall. When Delmar and I first met formally, I remember us being hesitant about one another. During practice, while conducting hitting drills, we looked across the field at each other distrustfully after smashing opposing teammates violently in practice. It was like we were trying to size each other up on the football field.

As time went on, Delmar and I began to talk more in practice and went to night clubs on the weekends. We talked uninterruptedly about football and how it impacted our lives. We were two Black males being recruited by top colleges across the country. We were impressed by each other's skill and ability. The "sizing up" of Delmar occurred when I observed how we constantly communicated with each other on and off the field about our playing skills. What impressed me about Delmar was his ability to engage in critical consciousness-raising dialogues about the game of football and relate it to our experiences as young Black males. Hence, our relationship grew immeasurably because I was just as conversational, passionate, and intellectual concerning football.

Most poignantly, after I injured my back in practice, Delmar talked to me about my disappointment and frustration. It was during this low point in my life that I had the pleasure to witness the power of Delmar's reverential dialogue. While at the hospital or conducting my physical training, Delmar counseled me about how the game of football was short-term and that it was important for me to continue my education regardless of my physical abilities or the coach's intent. In essence, Delmar's advice paid off because I now have my doctorate in education. For this reason, Delmar and I became friends because I was able to observe how he interacted with me, to be precise his ability to engage in critical consciousness-raising dialogues.

Listening.

When I was a child, I would love to sit and listen to my grandmother tell me stories about her life. My grandmother (mentioned above) was a proud Black woman who grew up in New Orleans, Louisiana. She was a stout, bow-legged lady who carried the weight of a million slaves on her back. She was the modern version of Harriet Tubman. I was honored to have known my grandmother, Cora, for my entire childhood and most of my adulthood. In addition to being a great storyteller, my grandmother was a devout listener. As different members of our family visited with her repeatedly every

Sunday, I was in awe of her ability to listen nonjudgmentally to their stories.

Many of my family members often complained to my grandmother about their failed marriages, experiences with school, and worldwide travel. As they told their stories, I watched my grandmother nod and peer into their eyes as if she was piercing their souls. My grandmother had this ability to listen until people exhausted themselves or became enlightened enough to resolve their own problems. As a result, I watched my family members leave my grandmother's house as changed people. In this way, her listening skills were transformative.

Likewise, after watching my grandmother listen astutely to my relatives, I developed a keen ability to listen and become cognizant of others' abilities to listen. Case in point, I met another best friend named Audrea while attending my doctoral program at the University of San Francisco. Audrea is a short, thin Caucasian woman who speaks prophetically, especially when talking about education. All through classes, we frequently exchanged brief glances after our intellectual remarks—at least we thought they were—concerning California's educational system.

As the program continued, Audrea and I would take long walks discussing various topics from educational policy to ineffective teaching. We both are California credentialed teachers who spent countless years in the classroom. What gained my respect for Audrea was her ability to listen. Audrea has an extraordinary ability to listen, similar to my grandmother's, in that she allows the speaker to feel respected, valued, and heard. I have discussed personal dilemmas with Audrea, sometimes talking for hours, where she has been unmoved by my passionate comments—she has literally stood still listening. Because of her remarkable skill in listening, I inaudibly declared Audrea as one of my best friends. Since my graduation from the program, Audrea and I have remained friends. Therefore, Audrea is one of my best friends because I have sized her up by her ability to listen—the same ability that I noticed in my grandmother as I grew up.

Because my mother and grandmother taught me how to observe and listen, I was able to develop a unique skill set, R.A.M., which has fueled my spirit for deepening my connection with the human beings I encounter. Hence, developing proficiency in observing and listening has allowed me to lay the groundwork for an authentic, bi-directional, trusting relationship to form between me and another individual.

The Delivery of R.A.M.

After the above stated genealogical experiences of R.A.M. took place within my life (i.e., the process of R.A.M. creation), I developed a process of R.A.M. implementation over the past 10 years in the form of a tool named the Horn Accountability Instrument (H.A.I.). Basically, the H.A.I. facilitates the delivery of R.A.M. by allowing people to establish and maintain focus throughout the course of their life, including (1) completing personal and professional goals and (2) creating a supportive and productive social network of R.A.M. affiliates (see Horn, 2010, for intricate details of H.A.I.).

R.A.M. delivery essentially involves the establishment of a genuine relationship between two human beings with or without an agenda. Once this relationship has been thoroughly solidified, then each individual, through authentic care and trust, begins creating goals that they both want to achieve. These goals should be thoroughly thought out, including a back-and-forth discussion, before the writing process begins. This detailed consideration and discussion of goals allows each human being to break apart the goals in order to accurately realize and articulate their true desires.

After goals have been discussed and written, each individual should complete a daily schedule to review the feasibility of time. This timeframe of goals allows people to achieve their goals based upon the availability of actual time. In essence, I have found that many people lack the skill of time management—inevitably impeding their movement towards personal and professional progress.

In Horn (2010), I endorse the importance of managing our limited weekly time allotment of 168 hours per any given week to perform our tasks. By maximizing these hours, I believe that all human beings can foster, develop and achieve all of their desired goals. Thus, I have created a way of engagement that has worked not only for me but for generations of family, friends, mentees and clients to stay focused and achieve their goals—the beauty of R.A.M. Once this process of human engagement and goal achievement is broken up into steps, one can witness the life-changing principles of R.A.M. I like to refer to this process as "Life-Long Mentoring."

Life-Long Mentoring is unparalleled to any type of mentoring I have observed over my life-span. My notion of life-long mentoring emerged after reading about one of my favorite heroines, Ms. Harriet Tubman, who assembled large quantities of slaves and navigated them toward freedom. Harriet Tubman freed over 300 slaves during a 10-year span. By this means, she held her people accountable to reach their goals by leading them to freedom. Thus, she dedicated her entire life for the cause of liberating an oppressed people.

Furthermore, I have observed many mentoring programs, declare that they are "true and faithful mentors." After observing these organizations fail at mentoring long-term, I came to understand that not all mentoring can be life-long because the reality is that many people succumb to their own personal failures, limitations, and shifted priorities. Conversely, a "Life-Long" mentor is someone who will commit to another human being from birth until death. In this way, I am trying to initiate the first social movement, since Harriet Tubman, where a dedicated group of committed human beings engage in a reciprocal process of holding people accountable through my concept of R.A.M.

To be precise, my process of life-long mentoring through R.A.M. has caused me to have a sense of urgency. For example, all of my accountability partners have inquired of me on several occasions, "Hey Aaron, what's up with your third book?" or "have you completed your hours for your marriage and family therapist (MFT) license exam?" (Researcher Journal, 2015). This simple checking-in process, a unique component to R.A.M., empowered me to achieve my goals of completing Book #3 and obtaining the 3,000 hours needed to qualify for my MFT exam. In essence, the constant checking-in process of R.A.M., either through face-to-face or other means, inspired my emotional intelligence in a way that moved my spirit toward progress.

To be exact, I was held accountable through my mentors' effective and persistent delivery of R.A.M.

Thus, I deem R.A.M. as one method to deepen human connection. Essentially, R.A.M. is a process that was developed over time. Formed in me from birth and further developed by influential processes, including (1) the resilience of my mother and grandmother, (2) my big brother's effective mentoring, (3) my influential rites of passage experiences and (4) my ability to silently reflect. These distinct processes cultivated my individual style of human relationship and connection, my concept of R.A.M., by making everyone feel valued and heard, holding people accountable to achieve their goals, and mentoring individuals through my one-on-one transparent coaching.

Dr. Horn's Use of R.A.M.

It is important for me to provide the reader with a streamlined version of R.A.M. not to oversimplify but to better understand this multifaceted and unique concept that I have crafted over the past 20 years. In order to understand the way in which I see the world (i.e., my R.A.M. lens), I will provide a brief process of how I use R.A.M. in my professional life. It is important to note that R.A.M. involves multiple belief systems, including African-centered belief of the Nguzo Saba, mentioned above, as well as other components that for the sake of time could not be included in this manuscript.

It is also important to disclose that R.A.M. is not a fixed methodology. It can occur in any order and at any time in a person's lifespan development. Most importantly, I have found that R.A.M. works best when the people who authentically engage in the R.A.M. relationship are genuinely concerned about enhancing the development of the person in whom they are relating. Hence, the fertile ground for successful R.A.M. implementation involves open-minded, genuine, caring, warm-hearted individuals who equally and reciprocally engage in an authentic R.A.M. relationship with one another.

Relationship.

As I describe in Horn (2012), my perception of human relationships involves connecting with people on a more profound spiritual level in an effort to help human beings become their best selves. In more specific terms, how can we as a human race make people feel better when we inhabit the same space? In African terms, I believe in unity (Umoja). I practice Umoja with everyone by always believing that we are intrinsically interconnected. By this means, I act as if and genuinely believe that all of the family, friends and colleagues I encounter come from the same womb as I did. This spiritual connectedness or inherent belief in unity allows for me to peek through the soul of the human being I am encountering.

Accountability.

Ujima (collective work and responsibility) explains my world view on accountability. I practice accountability by being consistent to the individuals who share my same space. In this way, I answer emails immediately, I return phone calls instantly, and I show up prepared and organized for my appointments on time and present (able to internalize the moment). I practice accountability to the core of my humanity. My ability to be accountable to my family, friends and clients has allowed me to make people feel better every time they leave my presence. Accountability is parallel to showing-up.

Mentoring.

I mentor using the African-centered principles of Kujichagulia (self-determination) and Nia (purpose). With all individuals, I encourage them by reminding them about being self-determined and being purpose-driven in life. Because my mentoring spirit was birthed in me through my parents, modeled and demonstrated by my grandmother, mother and brother, I naturally mentor my clients either as a teacher, counselor or coach. Therefore, my mentoring reveals itself through my unyielding spirit of encouragement.

And so, it is my hope that I paint a vivid picture for the reader of how R.A.M. can deepen human connection. For that reason, in the following chapters I present evocative representations of R.A.M., using the above-mentioned concepts, to illustrate the importance of deepening personal connections with human beings and inspire the reader to employ R.A.M. in daily interactions with others.

Reflection Questions for Chapter 1

These questions are intended to stimulate further consideration of the concepts introduced in the chapter and how they might apply in teaching, counseling, and other professional contexts.

1.   What aspects of R.A.M. do you recognize in your own lifespan development?

2.   How do you build relationships with your students, clients, or colleagues?

3.   In what ways do you hold your students, clients, or colleagues accountable for their actions and choices?

4.   How do you encourage your students, clients, or colleagues to hold each other accountable? What results have you observed?

5.   What does it mean to be a mentor—as the one who is mentoring and as the one who is being mentored?

6.   How does your current professional practice involve elements of R.A.M.?

7.   How might your current professional practice be enhanced by applying R.A.M.?

8.   In what ways would your students, clients, or colleagues benefit from a R.A.M.-inspired approach?

CHAPTER 2

BENEFITS OF THE R.A.M. VILLAGE

In this chapter, I disclose how I have personally and professionally benefited from what I call my R.A.M. village. In traditional African History the phrase, "it takes a village to raise a child," means that a child's nurturing is a communal effort. Thus, the pleasure and responsibility of child-raising extends beyond the biological family into a wider community. Specifically, everyone in the child's mental, spiritual and physical proximity is responsible for the child's upbringing. Similarly, I view R.A.M. relationships as the same. R.A.M. extends beyond the boundaries of a family's lineage. I have personally benefited from the R.A.M. village because I have been cared for, held accountable by and mentored by friends, family members and colleagues within and outside of my genealogical family. These individuals are known as my R.A.M. village.

Therefore, it is my intention to divulge how R.A.M. is a bi-directional process that I have profited from through engaging in authentic, R.A.M.-oriented relationships with my friends, family members, and current girlfriend. As a result, these relationships enhance my practice of R.A.M. The purpose of this chapter is for future mentees and mentors to understand how R.A.M. can have a significant impact on the individuals involved in the R.A.M. relationship. The following are portraits of my R.A.M. village relationships which demonstrate how I have benefited from these authentic and consistent relationships.

My Father's Straightforward R.A.M.

Although my father and I don't have a close relationship, I have always valued his straightforward R.A.M. After my parents divorced, my father would talk with my brother and me about being young Black men in America. My father Eli's straightforward or Nia-oriented (purpose) R.A.M. allowed me to grow into the empowered Black male I am today. When I was a teenager, I remember my father telling me with his firm voice, "Remember son.... white people will always look at you as a Nigger.... No matter how many degrees you have...They will always see you as less than..." (Researcher Journal, 2015).

Unfortunately, more often than not my father's straightforward warning came true. As mentioned throughout this book, I suffered many of the social injustices that my clients of color experience, especially institutional racism. My father's straightforward R.A.M. (i.e., candid advice about real life incidences of Black men) allowed me to be prepared for the various racialized obstacles that I would encounter in my life span. Unbeknownst to my father, his advice has fueled my passion to publish about the experiences that many Black men face growing up in mainstream America.

More specifically, my father's candid R.A.M. about being Black in America inspired me to develop my voice while working on my doctorate in graduate school. For instance, I wrote several papers and poems on the dehumanization of Black Americans (i.e., less than human) after conducting my initial research on my dissertation. Similar to what I wrote about in my poems, my research on slavery indicated that white slave owners devalued Black slaves in order to "use" them as chattel. This was also the reason for some white slave masters to brand the slaves. Black slaves were thus viewed as property (Bennett, 2003; Horn, 2010).

Consequently, when you devalue someone as "less than human" you do not have to see them as a connected being who belongs with you. This process of "devaluing" allows humans to disconnect from one another mentally, spiritually, emotionally and physically. More specifically, my father's candid R.A.M. empowered me as a Black man in America—reminding me that I can still be looked down upon as less than human. Conversely, I am empowered because my publications, teachings and respect in the field of education and counseling by all nationalities have allowed me to become one of the preeminent authorities on empowering young Black males. As a result, my publications allow for large scale macro-level conversations to occur regarding the healing process for the damage caused by the devaluation of African Americans. My father's candid R.A.M. has forever influenced my writing on Black male empowerment.

The Responsibility of Auntie Robey and Uncle Eddie

As stipulated in chapter 1, R.A.M. was birthed in me through my genealogy. As a young man, I benefited tremendously from my aunt's and uncle's steadfast love and childrearing. I have since interpreted their support of my mom in helping to raise me as responsible R.A.M. because they extended themselves beyond their family dynamic to assist with raising two boisterous young Black males who needed to be contained.

I remember like it was yesterday. When my mother and father were still married, Auntie Robey provided daycare for us and many other families within our Bay Area Black family network. Auntie Robey was and still is the pillar for many Black Bay Area families. Many Black families depended on Auntie Robey to provide quality daycare while they worked long hours to provide a stable environment for the children that Auntie Robey reared.

Many of my childhood friends and extended family were cultivated and nourished at Auntie Robey's daycare. Some of these extended family members included my cousin Malcolm, Andie, Jody, Kim and others, who were a stable part of my childhood identity. Many of these relationships lasted until my young adulthood. For many of us, Auntie Robey was the dependable disciplinarian who maintained the Black family values.

While our parents worked various types of employment to keep food on our tables, Auntie Robey provided a well-oiled machine of daycare including significant cultural components of the Black family. What other Black families missed, those who did not register their kids at Auntie Robey's, was the consistent discipline and the food. When the kids from Auntie Robey's acted out, and trust me we did, she disciplined us firmly and uncompromisingly.

When I was a young child, I was somewhat stubborn. I remember during one of my temper tantrums yelling aloud to Auntie Robey "fine...I won't eat" (Researcher Journal, 2015). What I didn't realize was Auntie Robey's unbending discipline. With her Jedi-like patience, she did not compromise or pay attention to my childish rants. As my stomach churned from hunger, I eventually recanted by gingerly asking Auntie Robey for a plate to eat. And of course, she allowed me to eat because she had plenty to spare.

Which leads me to my next favorite point of Auntie Robey's daycare—the food. From as early as I can remember, Auntie Robey could always cook. From her deliciously spicy fish dishes, to her tantalizing tasteful macaroni and cheese or even her plentiful assorted soup dishes, Auntie Robey could cook. Unlike most children, we were privy to feasting upon Auntie Robey's home-cooked meals every day. By this means, I recall Auntie Robey's R.A.M. as being family-oriented—embodying traditional Black family values.

Uncle Eddie's R.A.M. played a key role in my lifespan development. Although Auntie Robey helped to stabilize our family with her outstanding childcare child rearing, a divorce swiftly dismantled my parents' marriage. After the mandates of the divorce decree were settled, my mother was left to provide the teenage rearing of two highly energetic young Black males. And let me be the first to tell you, this was no easy undertaking.

To assist my mother, Uncle Eddie would often come by the house to check-in on us. I can clearly remember Uncle Eddie's voice as he marched into our bedrooms with his quiet yet strikingly fearful voice, "what's the problem?" he would sternly ask my brother and me. After a brief moment of dreadful reflection, we cautiously answered "nothing" in a low monotone voice. Nothing was wrong because we feared Uncle Eddie's retaliation of wrath upon us. In this sense, Uncle Eddie's R.A.M. allowed me to regain respect for the missing Black male authoritarian figure that used to be my father. Thus, my brother and I became beneficiaries of Uncle Eddie's authoritarian R.A.M. through his ability to show-up and be present in our lives.

The Steadfast Teachings of Uncle Danny

Uncle Danny has always been my teacher and mentor. His persistent teaching has allowed me to grow into the teacher I am today. As early as I can recall, Uncle Danny has always taught me about life. One of his classic teachings involved my paychecks, including putting ten percent away for me first and then putting the rest in my bank account for a rainy day. The purpose for this 10% teaching was to put the first portion of my earnings away for me to do whatever I wanted (e.g., go to a movie, buy a CD, etc.) and then I was to use the rest of my earnings for personal responsibilities. At this time in my life, I did not have any rent or credit cards, but I was able to start a savings account for the remaining 90% of my earnings.

Even more, I can recall Uncle Danny's life skills teaching like it was yesterday. I was listening to Uncle Danny teach as I stood taut, absorbing every word. I was a young, hard-headed (stubborn) high school teenager who felt that I had command of the entire world. Uncle Danny stands about six feet and some change tall and speaks with a commanding voice. I remember Uncle Danny inspiring me in his usual authoritative tone stating, "Aaron...remember when you get your check...put ten percent away for you, then put the rest away in your savings..." (Researcher Journal, 2015). This lesson has never left my mind ever since Uncle Danny spoke their existence into my life.

As I grew into a young adult, I took Uncle Danny's paycheck principle of "paying myself first" in all practices of employment. For instance, I remember working as a young automotive warehouse attendant for a local automotive organization in the Bay Area. I was so happy and excited to receive my first check from this company, when all of a sudden, I could hear the whispers of Uncle Danny's voice haunting my every gaze at this insignificant piece of financial exchange. As I sauntered to the bank, Uncle Danny's words became more lucid in my cerebral cortex – pay me first! I then realized that it was time to put aside ten percent for me and the rest in my savings. And I did just that! After paying my rent and credit card bills with my ninety percent, I used my ten percent to attend some movies and buy music, my favorite treat to myself. Looking back on this moment, what inspired me then and what continues to inspire me today is Uncle Danny's faithful reminder to pay myself first. Uncle Danny has always been a profound teacher in my life and continues to be one of my most persistent mentors.

Auntie Paulette's Hustle Spirit

Following right behind Uncle Danny's zeal for teaching is the hustle spirit of my Auntie Paulette, Uncle Danny's beloved wife. Akin to Uncle Danny, Auntie Paulette is another teacher and mentor. Her Nia (purpose) spirit has influenced my life in so many ways, especially always having a hustle (i.e., multiple jobs and opportunities). When I was a young boy, I would hang out with my auntie Paulette on the weekends at her home. These weekends were some of the best times in my childhood because my Auntie Paulette demonstrated in her spirit those same encouraging words that Uncle Danny would say—invest in yourself, nephew! By investing in myself, my auntie wanted me to always have multiple jobs and projects because she believed in staying employed. And just like to Uncle Danny's Nia-driven advice I listened and observed!

I have always kept multiple jobs and consulting projects. Even when I was in college, I had numerous jobs and various occupational ventures that kept me employed and busy. My auntie wanted me to stay employed because she believed in living a purpose-driven life of employment and business. For example, when I was in high school, I remember my auntie paying me to take care of odd jobs around her house and her business. Both she and my Uncle Danny owned property that I helped maintain. Little did my auntie and uncle know, but helping them on the weekends would be the most influential support they could offer me, particularly at this stage and development in my lifespan.

Santrock (2009) reminds us that during the stages of adolescent development (i.e., ages 10 to 12 and 18 to 21), identity development accumulates to a point where an individual is able to consciously reflect upon the psychosocial, physical, and emotive development that are essential to identity. Nonetheless, adolescent identity development involves experimentation. In this way, I was able to reflect upon my Auntie Paulette's spirit and example of having multiple hustling, internalizing its importance in my life. Because of Auntie Paulette's example, I have never been without employment for extended periods of time nor have I become dependent on one employer as my sole provider of income. Auntie Paulette empowered me by teaching me the significance of always having multiple hustles—financial flexibility and stability.

Auntie Lise's Live-One-Day-At-A-Time Mantra

Auntie Lise is one of those aunts who you always love to be around. Her personality is jovial and her temperament is joyous. Like many of my aunts, Auntie Lise helped my mom raise me while I was growing up and I will never forget the way she instilled in me her belief to live one-day-at-a-time. When I was in college, I remember my aunt and me hanging out into the late hours of the night. Lise was the aunt who I partied with after she baby-sat me years earlier. Lise and I would travel the streets of San Francisco painting the town Black. We attended every club, party scene and hip hop joint that San Francisco had to offer. During this stage of my life span development (mid-twenties), I was continuing to develop my identity as a strong Black male playing football and exploring various employment options.

Auntie Lise fit in perfectly with this stage of my development because I was partying and having fun—things that most mid-twenties young folk often do at this stage of their life. I can recall when I would converse with Auntie Lise about various subjects in life, I remember auntie stating, "Live your life nephew….have fun…live one-day-at-a-time…." (Researcher Journal, 2015). This mantra has stayed with me all of my life because when I often face some serious road blocks, I can hear the subtle words of my Auntie Lise resonating within me. My auntie's one-day-at-a-time mentality has helped me navigate some recent trials and tribulations that I faced. Case in point, I recently accumulated my mandated hours (3,000) for my Marriage and Family Therapy license for the state of California. Because this three-year-long task included internships that focused on child and family trauma and almost devoured my soul, I needed to take a break before studying for my test.

After considering my various employment options and other responsibilities, I heeded the words of my auntie to live one-day-at-a-time and decided to resign from the internship because of my trauma fatigue. My aunt's words of wisdom helped me to resign from this internship and take a break because I was not living one-day-at-a-time.

I was so focused on building my skills as a therapist that I forgot about my physical, spiritual and mental health. My aunt's mantra helped me to slow down my thought processes and remember the importance of putting myself first, just like what Uncle Danny and Auntie Paulette taught me. Because of my Auntie Lise, I am currently living a one-day-at-a-time lifestyle, rebuilding my physical, mental and spiritual self back to their normal healthy state of being.

My Auntie Jan's Love and Laughter

My Auntie Jan is a beautiful caramel-colored Black woman who helped my mother raise me and my brother. She has always been there for me, and I will never forget her perpetual love and boisterous laughter. Because of these two beautiful gifts that Auntie Jan has generously shared with me over the years, I can cope with severe trauma and misfortune. One of the most reflective memories regarding my aunt's unending love was when I was in an unhealthy relationship with a woman, whom I was about to marry, from a church I attended when I was 28 years old. This woman had a plan to send money from my bank account in an attempt to finance herself, her ex-husband, and her entire family. After some extensive research and counseling from Auntie Jan, the wedding never materialized. Therefore, my auntie saved me from a destructive marriage and financial catastrophe. I love my aunt because she is always by my side, especially during distressful normative and non-normative life transitions.

One of the most well-known personal attributes is my Auntie Jan's humor. As my aunt and I discuss stressful life experiences, we often burst into laughter because she has always had a humorous outlook on life. For example, she and I often mimic and make fun of the various unexpected life events that we encounter on a daily basis. I fondly remember retelling a story to Auntie Jan about a trip to Disney World, which I took with my mentee and his mother many years ago. On the flight back home (Orlando to San Francisco), the plane's air conditioning system caught fire in mid-air. Although I was extremely terrified during this horrific event, I retold the story to Auntie Jan using humor. I can still remember Auntie Jan's infamous breathless laugh as she looked me directly in my face laughing hysterically. Her impromptu laughter thus triggered me to laugh uncontrollably as well.

Thus, by using humor with Auntie Jan, retelling the horrendous events that occurred on the plane, I was able to de-escalate and minimize the potential long-lasting impact of trauma that could be lingering within my subconscious.

Auntie Jeannie's Loyalty

Auntie Jeannie is the aunt who always showed up in my life. My Auntie Jeannie's role in my life was parallel to Ujima (collective work and responsibility). As a young child, I remember Auntie Jeannie at my grandmother's house helping around the house during holidays and birthdays. Although Auntie Jeannie is not my biological aunt, I have always thought of her as my biological aunt. I love Auntie Jeannie because she was always there in my life – always showing up. Her loyalty to our family is mind-blowing. When you needed someone to help out around the house, Auntie Jeannie was always there. When you needed someone to help coordinate a holiday or birthday party, Auntie Jeannie was always there helping in any way she could. When you needed someone to babysit, Auntie Jeannie babysat for all of the children in the family, especially me and my brother.

My Auntie Jeannie's Ujima's spirit was very present when she babysat me and my brother. In fact, I commend auntie on dealing with our intense personalities. As mentioned earlier, I was a boisterous young child. Always into everything I could lay my hands on. I distinctly remember one babysitting session with Auntie Jeannie where I would test her Ujima spirit. It was early one morning when my aunt was cooking me and brother grits (a processed hot cereal). I was bored, so I figured in order to entertain myself I scooped up some of the piping hot grits with a spoon and started splattering them on the ceiling. I thought it was fun because I was using the spoon like a sling-shot, sending the grits spiraling out of control in the air until they reached the ceiling in a chaotic pattern of mess. When my aunt reappeared in the kitchen, all I can remember is my aunt giving me the business (code for discipline). What was most memorable was her attitude after the incident. Auntie Jeannie never shamed me for the incident. In fact, she used humor in retelling the incident and continued to babysit me and my brother. Now that's the true spirit of Ujima!

Craig and Chris's Cultural R.A.M.

Chris and Craig have been a part of my life span development for years. Both have encouraged me through their cultural style of R.A.M., particularly through demonstrating Umoja (unity) and Nia (purpose) with me for over 20 years. All three of us grew up in San Francisco, sharing one common purpose—playing junior college sports for City College of San Francisco. Although Craig and Chris are blood brothers, we were all related through our cultural selves—young Black male athletes navigating the streets of San Francisco.

Like many young Black males growing up in the 1980's, we encountered prejudice, microaggressions, institutional racism and other forms of racism in our daily lives. Most horrendous, I was called a nigger by white people on numerous occasions. For all three of us, these brief encounters with racism can have long-lasting effects on our psyche, especially feelings of dehumanization and being devalued. Hardy (2012) refers to these feelings of being devalued as, "….a direct by-product of racism, inextricably linked to the deification of whiteness and the demonization of non-white hues. It is perpetrated throughout society, including in the very systems with the stated mission of serving youth…" (p. 25). Although my self-esteem was high because of my importance to the CCSF football team, I struggled internally with feelings of being devalued by a larger white society that existed within San Francisco.

Consequently, Craig and Chris's practice of Umoja and Nia served as a buffer to thwart these injustices to my cultural self. More than often, Craig and Chris would engage me in cultural dialogues which boosted my cultural confidence and sense of purpose in life. When we would gather, all of our conversations dealt with the current racial and cultural injustices that were occurring to Black San Franciscans, especially the impact of gentrification. Because of our cultural conversations, I was able to successfully navigate personal and professional situations that impacted me racially.

For instance, one evening Chris and I were hanging out at a night club during our years as star CCSF athletes. Chris was a phenomenal CCSF basketball player and I was an upcoming linebacker. As we both relished our athletic achievements, we were both quickly reminded of our dehumanizing value to San Francisco. As we walked to our cars, after a night out on the town, a white cab driver approached us and shouted, "Get out of the street you fucking niggers." I was infuriated with rage and began to chase down the cab when Chris grabbed me threw me onto the car calming down with his soothing voice. I remember him eloquently and gently whispering to me, "...You gotta chill Big Horn... You gotta chill..." (Researcher Journal, 2015).

As we reflected on this incident later that evening, Chris reminded me that we as student athletes have to watch ourselves because young and older athletes look up to us as role models. Many other people from CCSF had been out with us that evening and Chris reminded me that people are always watching us. Chris also reminded me of our purpose (Nia) that evening in that we are more than just mere college athletes. No, Chris emphatically reminded me that we represent the many young Black males who are not privileged to attend college because they had been unnecessarily killed or excessively incarcerated or they struggle with substance abuse. Similar to the incident with my grandmother and my hair, Chris reminded me of the larger purpose of my life—to represent Black America with pride. Without minimizing the impact of the white cab driver's actions, Chris used his Nia and Umoja attitude to encourage me about being a prideful Black man; in this sense, turning the other cheek for the greater good of Black America.

Similarly, Uncle Craig uses his Nia (purpose) spirit with me as a means to keep me focused. Before Uncle Craig was my Uncle (through marriage), he was my football coach at CCSF. During these years, I fondly remember Uncle Craig (i.e., Coach Craig) teaching me various life skills lessons, especially encouraging me to continue my studies in the library. As an active testosterone-filled male, I astutely listened to Coach Craig's advice—just like listening to a financial consultant for a reputable high-ranking investment company. His advice was always purpose-driven and no-nonsense. I believe Coach Craig also saw in me an educationally driven person as he coached the basic skills of junior college football.

As we engaged in various critical conscious dialogues on the cold and wet football field at CCSF, Coach Craig entwined his personal life as a former collegiate athlete along with his challenges as a Black man growing up in mainstream America. I loved every bit of his story telling, especially the stories that involved how he navigated institutional racism. All in all, Uncle Craig lovingly instilled Black pride in me! His story telling and life skills dialogue helped me to become a proud Black male – Dr. Aaron Lamont Horn. In fact, I often reflect upon Uncle Craig's frequent shrieks to me across the dinner table at family gatherings (i.e., a sign of pride in is nephew), "It's your world Doctor!" (Researcher Journal, 2015).

Marlena's Gentle Encouragement

Some Christians believe that humans can represent or possess qualities of an Angel (a spiritual being). By this definition, my cousin Marlena has an Angelical spirit. As long as I have known my cousin Marlena, all my entire life, she has always been genuinely caring and loving. She loves without boundaries and limits. She cares for every person she encounters as if they were her biological family (i.e., R.A.M. spirit). Marlena encourages you so that you make the necessary improvements in your life without asking for additional help. In this way, Marlena's advice is life-altering R.A.M. Most noticeably, when you need advice and help from cousin Marlena she is always willing to extend herself, especially offering encouragement in the most gentle and loving way. Marlena's most unforgettable act of kindness occurred to me when I was meeting with her years ago discussing the formulation and growth of my consulting company (Horn Development Consulting - HDC).

As Marlena met with me, it was like listening to a preacher, evangelist and priest all at the same time. Over the course of an hour, Marlena spoke into my spirit, breathing expectation, joy and excitement. She quietly discussed how HDC would eventually grow and prosper as long as I spent time building each component of the business. She also encouraged me to continue my writing, making sure I always had a case of books with me at all times because she wanted me to be prepared, just like my big brother, for life's unexpected opportunities. A couple of years later, Marlena's advice and gentle encouragement paid off. I was attending a local Baptist church in the Bay View one Sunday morning, when all of a sudden the preacher began referencing my work during his sermon. The preacher discussed, "And Dr. Horn knows about the tough life that some of these Black boys live...He knows because he writes about their lives...He works with young Black boys every day." (Researcher Journal, 2015).

By the time the sermon had ended, I had a plethora of Black church attendees huddling around me asking about my books and buying my latest publication (*I Got'Cho Back*) on the spot. I had to run to my car and shuffle through my trunk to pull out the remaining books I had been selling the previous week. Marlena's gentle advice of always being ready as a publisher paid off in dividends because at that particular unexpected moment in time, Dr. Horn was ready. Even though many of my books had been sold previously, I was ready to sell the remaining books I had stored in the trunk of my car. Cousin Marlena's gentle encouragement allowed me to make a life-altering (i.e., do-it-now R.A.M.) adjustment to always be ready as a published author and business owner.

Reggie's Strategic Thinking

My fraternity brother and best friend Reggie has influenced my personal and professional career over the past 20 years. Reggie's Nia-R.A.M. friendship (purpose) has influenced me to make strategic career moves in my life. I met Reggie 20 years ago when we were students at San Francisco State (SFSU). At the time, Reggie was already an Alpha man who had been groomed partly by the university but mostly by his own intellect to move intentionally throughout the academic system. Reggie was actually the one who invited me to join Alpha Phi Alpha, eventually leading me through the entire process. Reggie inspired me because of his premeditated guidance within his professional career. When Reggie contemplated, he was making plans for five years down the road.

For instance, Reggie eventually left SFSU to pursue other student services and leadership opportunities, which was his specialty, across the country down south. What followed this appointment was a successful career as a program developer, representing underserved students, for universities. Reggie, otherwise known as Dr. Stewart, is currently working for the University of Nevada as the Chief Diversity Officer (CDO). I view Reggie's current position and professional standing as a compliment to his renowned ability to think strategically. As a testament to his thinking, Reggie influenced me to join the elite paratroopers of the US Military. After finishing my bachelors and master's degrees at SFSU, I was contemplating my next professional transition. Thinking in terms as my mentor, Reggie, I thought five years ahead.

In five years, I wanted to have my own health benefits and have my initial college loans from my bachelors and master's degrees paid off in full. The only option at the time that offered that type of comprehensive compensation was joining the United States Army. After discussing this option with my family, I joined the army and upon graduation from basic training, the army began paying off my student loans in large lump sums. In addition, after a successful and honorable discharge (an official positive departure from the military), I now have full medical benefits, in addition to other resources, for the rest of my life. I credit my positive military experience, especially my medical benefits and loan repayments, in part to Reggie for modeling his ability to think critically.

Rob's Loyalty

My best friend and most reliable accountability partner is Robert Lucas. I have known Robert since I was in high school. I met him through my brother Eli because he and Rob attended the same high school in San Francisco. What stands out the most about Rob is his loyalty. As my accountability partner for over five years, he has been committed to the process of R.A.M. check-ins, not missing one weekly or monthly check-in. As a result of Rob's loyalty he has rebirthed in me the spirit of Nehemiah from the Bible (Old Testament). Akin to Nehemiah's desire to rebuild his community, I want to rebuild the community of underserved families through a spirit of R.A.M. loyalty. For this reason, Rob's demonstration of loyalty over the past five years has reawakened a spirit of R.A.M. loyalty within me.

Jeff's Relaxed Spirit

Jeff, my former supervisor, has become a part of my extended family since our friendship began several years ago. I have known Jeff for over 10 years in both a personal and professional capacity. Jeff is the CEO of Brainstorm, the organization that changed my life just like R.A.M. I first met Jeff 13 years ago in an extension class at a local Bay Area college. I was fresh out of the United States Army and eager to sharpen my educational skills. After Jeff and I talked briefly in class, we became professional associates. Jeff offered me a position within his company as an educational consultant.

Over the next 13 years, I would learn from one of the most intellectual educators and counselors of the Bay Area. As I worked with the children and families who were referred to me through Jeff, I further developed R.A.M. by helping these children and their families accomplish personal and professional goals. Through our professional and personal R.A.M.-infused relationship, Jeff taught me how to relax as a provider. Throughout many candid conversations, I was able to learn how to carefully evaluate the needs of underserved children and families while relaxing throughout the entire process. In this way, Jeff taught me how to infuse self-care with R.A.M.

Belinda's Committed Friendship

Every now and then God inserts people into your life, I call them Angels, to guide you along your journey. One of those Angels, who is coincidently one of my best friends, is Belinda. A strong and courageous Latina, Belinda is the premiere advocate for Latino Social Justice and Human Rights in the Bay Area. I met Belinda through a mutual colleague when I was a graduate student.

Similar to my best friend Eric, Belinda and I hit it off immediately through our shared interest of serving underserved families. Belinda is a staunch believer in freedom and equality for underserved families and so am I. I have benefitted tremendously from my friendship with Belinda due to our R.A.M.-motivated friendship. Because of Belinda's motivational spirit, I have been able to remain in the field of counseling, developing my own culturally aware type of therapy.

Where do I begin describing my friendship with Belinda? Over the past five years, Belinda has been the best support system ever. Belinda has been by my side throughout some of my darkest times, especially after my grandmother died in 2011. Belinda walked with me through my spiritual journey as I tried to reconcile my place in the field of counseling while grieving the loss of my grandmother. The type of friendship that Belinda demonstrates to me and to her other friends is priceless. In fact, Belinda's steadfast relationship has helped to stabilize thousands of undocumented families throughout the Bay Area. Belinda's passion for raising the critical consciousness and voices of the often silenced undocumented family has had a resounding impact on the Latino population as a whole in California.

Even more, Belinda's committed relationship showed up in a Nia (purpose) spiritual sense. Whenever we talked weekly, Belinda would remind me of my purpose in life, especially to make people feel better. When I was struggling with staying in the field of counseling, Belinda motivated me by reminding me of the many people who informed her about how I inspired them. Many of these people were colleagues of Belinda's, people whom I had forgotten I mentored, who spoke highly of my ability to motivate, inspire and enhance their self-esteem. Belinda checked-in with me every week for an entire year, discussing our personal and professional goals. Her committed relationship allowed me to continue my drive and passion for completing the masters in counseling, eventually completing my mandated hours in the field of marriage and family therapy.

Belinda's relationship embodies R.A.M. because she has the unique ability to stand faithfully and consistently when the lives of her precious friends instantaneously disrupt into chaos. This is where Belinda does her best work. As a result of her unwavering friendship, she has resuscitated and revived many of her friends back from the depths of hell. In this way, I have benefited from Belinda's R.A.M.-driven friendship through her untiring support. When I wanted to quit the field of counseling, Belinda was there for me. When I could not stop crying over my grandmother's death, Belinda was there for me. As I successfully navigate the field of counseling, Belinda is here with me. As a result of Belinda's R.A.M., I have completed my required counseling intern hours for pre-licensure.

Eddie's Attunement

Eddie is another best friend who has held me accountable over the past five years with his attentive listening and nonjudgmental friendship. Similar to so many of my best friends already mentioned, Eddie and I met while attending a counseling psychology program at a local Bay Area University. We initially met each other in classes that we had over the two years that I attended the graduate program. Ultimately, Eddie and I deepened our friendship after we both realized we were attuned to the value of meaningful conversation and relationship.

What has occurred over the past five years as friends has been nothing less than excellent. Eddie's open-minded, R.A.M.-enthused friendship has allowed me to discuss my feelings openly about being lonely and isolated within a newly developed and gentrified city of San Francisco. In short, I have been able to freely express my frustration to Eddie of living in a city where I have become invisible. Through his persistent active listening and being attuned to my feelings, Eddie allowed for my voice to be heard and validated. As a result, Eddie's R.A.M. helped me to navigate and eventually overcome a distressing time in my life.

The best part about being friends with Eddie is that when we meet, we can't stop talking. In fact, we usually end up talking until the sun sets. We talk as if we were distant brothers living on opposite sides of the coast. Eddie and I are friends because when we first met each other, we talked and listened to one another with reverence. And five years later, we still have the same respect for each other's voice. I have benefited from Eddie's R.A.M. by discussing my innermost concerns. In this way, Eddie's R.A.M. helped to free my spirit, where the heart of R.A.M. lies, from unwanted stress and tribulation.

Maurice's Nonjudgment Listening

Maurice is a friend who has been dear to my heart for 20 years. We met as young academics during my tenure at San Francisco State University (SFSU) as a student and employee of the Equal Opportunity Program. Maurice (aka Mo) is a human being who captures a room with his smile. After several years of friendship, Mo and I lost touch when I joined the military. Shortly after my honorable discharge in 2003, we reconnected again at SFSU. This time, we were both refueling and retooling our shared passion for academia and scholarship.

As we began to reconnect, I remembered what I enjoyed about Mo's friendship—his unwavering ability to listen. In fact, Mo's listening skills have helped me to overcome some of my most troubling personal and professional struggles. For example, I remember when I first re-registered for SFSU. I was fresh out of the US Army and feeling that my academic skills were diminished. I was having difficulty transitioning from military to civilian life.

As I ranted about my transition, Mo intelligently and intensely listened without talking. After several days of indirect ranting, I noticed a change in my demeanor. My ranting ceased and I became more proactive about solutions that would ultimately ease my military-civilian life transition. Through the process, I benefited from Mo's attentive listening of R.A.M. by feeling heard, acknowledged and valued. Mo and I continue to talk every month during our monthly check-ins, discussing both personal and professional struggles. In the same way, Mo continues to listen attentively.

Momma Page's Authenticity

Momma Page is yet another human being who personifies the beauty of R.A.M. so effortlessly. I met Momma Page a couple of years ago while working at a non-profit in San Francisco. Almost immediately, I was captured by her authenticity, which she wears on her sleeve. Throughout our years as colleagues, friends and now extended family, Momma Page has always been direct and straightforward. Momma Page's authenticity has impacted my life because I have improved my ability to be straightforward with the people in my life, especially my R.A.M. affiliates. In this way, Momma Page's authenticity has made me become more authentic with my R.A.M. delivery.

For instance, I was recently asked by a local social service agency to provide volunteer services for a former client. In the past, I would have easily accepted volunteer employment based on my eagerness to serve others. After being exposed to Momma Page's authentic spirit of boundaries and straightforwardness, I was able to firmly, but gently, decline this offer. In this way, my personal style of R.A.M. has improved by becoming more forthright with people—improving my personal and professional boundaries immensely.

Cecil's Desire for Human Vulnerability

Cecil is a friend who has held me accountable over the last five years. As a professional life coach and faithful Christian, Cecil is a one-in-a-lifetime friend because of his devotion to his wife and children. Akin to Belinda, Cecil is another one of God's Angels. Cecil and I met five years ago at a local San Francisco gymnasium. As we both worked out, we would give each other the male head nod, indicating that we respectfully acknowledged each other's presence. After days of eye contact and head nodding, we approached each other to discuss our affinity with the gym and the city at large. Instantaneously, God blessed me with yet another friend.

As Cecil and I began meeting for coffee, we both discovered that we had a passion to be closer with God, and we desired deeper commitments, responsibility and relationship with other human beings. Cecil intricately describes this process as humans becoming more vulnerable with one another. Vulnerability is one of the key concepts to healthy relationship building or unity (Umoja). On any given day, Cecil defines this vulnerability as informing others about your strengths and weaknesses—letting people see beyond your titles and accolades. I agree wholeheartedly with Cecil on the importance of becoming more vulnerable.

Because of Cecil's R.A.M.-related coaching, including his desire for human beings to become more vulnerable with each other, I have become more willing to be vulnerable. As Cecil and I met throughout the years, we held each other accountable to achieving our personal and professional goals. Cecil and I would check-in at least once a month as a necessary process of R.A.M. permeation. Through our monthly check-ins, I have been able to identify personal and professional vulnerable goals that have allowed me to grow in all aspects of my life. By vulnerable goals, I mean both Cecil and I discussed how each of us wanted to become more vulnerable in our personal lives with the people we encountered. For me, before I met Colette, I wanted to have more candid conversations with women. I wanted to open myself up to some of my female friends and talk about things that I do not normally share, especially my personal and professional goals. This type of vulnerability was important to me at this time in my life because I had recently shut down emotionally due to a bad break-up with an ex-girlfriend.

This "shutting down" emotionally caused me to miss out on opportunities to converse with potential people whom I could date, minimizing the natural exploration process of dating. After meeting with Cecil on a weekly basis, talking through my short-lived process of shutting down, I was able to rebuild my self-confidence in talking more candidly to women. As I began having discussions with female friends, I was smitten by a young lady named Colette (see below) whereupon I would talk endlessly about personal and professional goals as if we were married for 20 years. As a result, Cecil's desire for humans to become more vulnerable resulted in my eventual yearning to be more open and candid with female friends and falling in love.

My Dearly Beloved Colette

My heart is full with joy and satisfaction because I met my equally yoked life partner—Ms. Colette Ann Marie Reid. In June of 2014 my life changed forever when I met my dearly beloved. Resembling my mother, Colette is a statuesque African Queen with strong morals and values. Her countenance reeks of respect. When I met Colette, I knew I had met my life partner. As our eyes met at first glance, we both smiled as if we knew something that nobody in the entire world knew.

A year later, my life has changed drastically because of Colette's unwavering, love-embodied R.A.M. Colette's R.A.M. has allowed me to feel like the most important person in the world. Her love for me has been like no other—always encouraging, communicative and prayerful. My beloved is a "praying fool" as we say in the Black community. She prays persistently and unceasingly. I love everything about her, but her ability to pray endlessly is the number one reason why I fell in love with her.

I distinctly fell in love with Colette because her heart is pure and by pure I mean open, vulnerable and unselfish. And so I say to the world, thank you God for sending me a praying woman. Because of my beloved's Godly R.A.M., I have begun the process of deepening my relationship with God. I am so thankful that God has partnered me with someone who desires mankind to be at their best every day. I look forward to praying with my beloved every day for the rest of our lives. I love you Colette Ann Marie Reid.

These are only a few of the relationships that inspire, encourage and motivate me to become a better human being and achieve my goals. Because I was able to deepen my connection with these individuals, I continue to hone my skills of R.A.M. Consequently, my connections to my family members, friends and girlfriend allow me to remain humble in the presence of other human beings who benefit from the human connection of R.A.M.

Reflection Questions for Chapter 2

1. As illustrated in the preceding examples, R.A.M. relationships benefit both participants. Describe some of the specific ways in which you and others have benefited from your relationships.

2. How do you recognize and value the benefits that you are receiving and providing in your relationships?

3. What are some ways that R.A.M. relationships can include students, clients, or colleagues who typically might be excluded, marginalized, or dehumanized?

4. If you have a student, client, or colleague who is struggling with discouraging challenges, how might the elements of R.A.M. be employed to encourage and support that person?

5. In what specific ways can a R.A.M.-aligned approach help students, clients, or colleagues meet expectations and achieve goals?

6. As relationships form and grow, community is developed. What might be some unique benefits of a community built on R.A.M. relationships?

CHAPTER 3

PORTRAITS OF R.A.M.

In this chapter, I discuss how R.A.M. has influenced my friends, family, extended family members and clients over the past 20 years. Clients' names have been changed to protect their confidentiality. My hope is to paint a picture of how R.A.M., when used appropriately, can be influential in changing the lives of human beings.

Kenny's Transition

One of my best friends, whom I have known for over 10 years, is Kenny. Kenny is a powerful attorney and doctor of education. As one of Kenny's closest friends, I have coached him in several areas of his life, especially professional development. Kenny is a highly gifted individual, especially in the areas of disability law and Latino studies. I value my friendship with Kenny because he has been continually consistent with using R.A.M. to empower himself and others.

Case in point, after Kenny passed the California Bar Exam, he pursued his lifelong dream of becoming a doctoral student, focusing on Latino studies. During this transition, Kenny sought me out for specific advice regarding his transition from attorney to educator. I coached Kenny using R.A.M. to help him identify his long-term goals and objectives, post-doctoral degree. Since completing his doctoral thesis, Kenny has become a published author, a government official, and a high-powered legal consultant. Kenny has disclosed to me on several occasions that my R.A.M. coaching improved his professional development by helping him to identify and obtain specific goals and objectives related to his blended career of law and education.

Relationship.

When Kenny discusses how R.A.M. impacted his professional development (i.e., breaking R.A.M. apart), he elaborated that my authentic relationship with him allowed him to feel empowered to redevelop his professional skill sets. He discussed that he has always been appreciative of my non-judgmental manner towards him. In this way, I used Umoja (unity) and Nia (purpose) with Kenny to authentically foster my relationship with him (Wilson, 1991). Thus, my friendship with Kenny was almost destined to occur because when I first met him I observed him to be a genuinely kind-hearted person with purpose and drive so our friendship paralleled our personal beliefs of unity and purpose.

Accountability.

In addition, Kenny also describes that the most important transition of his professional development occurred through our process of being accountable to each other. Kenny constantly acknowledges me in emails and phone conversations about my ability to hold him accountable to his goals. For instance, when Kenny drafted his letter of intent when he was applying for doctoral graduate schools, I would make specific editorial comments to increase the influence of his letter. Kenny remained accountable to this process by making adjustments to his letter and meeting with me on a weekly basis to ensure proper editorial progress.

Mentoring.

Even more, Kenny confides in me often that my mentoring has allowed him to grow personally and professionally in many ways. In Kenny's view, the mentoring process of R.A.M. involves my monthly check-ins and meet ups that I engaged in with Kenny. It also involved my giving him highly edited examples of my writing to review when he needed assistance in writing a letter of interest or even writing a graduate school level paper. Similar to Wilson's (1991) Afrikan-centered Educational Rehabilitation techniques, I mentored Kenny using these same principles which included, (1) using our trusting relationship to enhance his self-esteem about being an effective graduate school student, (2) reinforcing his heritage (i.e., Latin American) as a strength to utilize within his work as a doctoral student and (3) using cooperative and communal practices to assist Kenny with competing his college assignments.

Eric's Consistency

Another one of my dearest friends, Eric, has also discussed positive benefits from my R.A.M.-inspired coaching. I have known Eric for over five years. I met him as a graduate student when we were both studying for the master's in counseling psychology. As soon as we were introduced by a former professor, Eric and I immediately connected to one another. Part of why we connected so firmly and quickly was that we were two "out of place" Black males in a predominately white University.

Relationship.

Eric and I formed our relationship mainly because we both are interested in counseling young Black males to help them feel better about themselves. We both have various shared passions in common. Among many of his academic passions, Eric is interested in the betterment of young Black males. In particular, Eric enjoys counseling Black males who struggle with substance abuse issues. This type of high-risk counseling is second nature to Eric. As we developed our friendship, Eric often made an effort to connect with me on a weekly basis to further our newly motivated friendship. As Eric reflects upon our friendship, he has often disclosed that he appreciated my Nguzo Saba spirit, especially my Umoja (unity), Kujichagulia (self-determination), Ujima (collective work), Nia (purpose), Kuumba (creativity) and Imani (faith) (Wilson, 1991).

On most occasions, I have used Umoja, Nia and Imani with Eric to solidify and maintain our friendship. Similar to Kenny, Eric is also thoughtful and honest. As I began to meet with Eric weekly, I began to foster a relationship that was based upon the above-mentioned principles to help Eric enhance his self-esteem and personal trust in himself to become an efficient graduate student in a doctor of psychology program—Eric's most important passion concerning how to better serve young Black males. Thereby, Eric believes that our relationship inevitably helped him to apply for and become accepted into a local doctorate of psychology program.

Accountability.

As Eric delved into his graduate program, we often met at least once a month to discuss his school work and future objectives. Eric progressed well as a graduate student. He obtained a high grade point average, performed well on class presentations and began developing his graduate study research skills. Shortly after graduation, Eric and I began furthering our relationship to target specific professional goals that he desired, namely his doctorate degree.

Over the course of the next two years, Eric and I intensified our relationship by including monthly coaching sessions (ala accountability and mentoring) to target his academic goals and focus on applying for Bay Area graduate school programs. Our monthly check-ins included editing Eric's graduate letters of intent, discussions about potential graduate school programs that may or may not be a good fit and preparing him for his potential acceptance into a doctoral program. As we met, Eric and I both were accountable to each other. As I mentored him on how to write letters of intent, he accepted my advice and followed up with specific editing that immediately enhanced his writing. Eric and I maintained our accountability to one another, meeting face-to-face or by phone, until Eric's writing and graduate school preparation improved. Unique to this process was Eric's commitment to our R.A.M. relationship. Eric has been accountable and responsible (Ujima) over the past three years and has remained accountable ever since. Because of our reciprocal accountability, Eric has been accepted into a well-renown Doctorate of Psychology program and is currently preparing to meet his fall 2015 commencement goal.

Mentoring.

Eric often credits my mentoring as having had a direct impact on his doctoral application preparation and acceptance into a doctoral program. Throughout the course of our R.A.M. relationship, I have mentored Eric using various Nguzo Saba components, particularly with Kujichagulia (self-determination). I have encouraged Eric to complete all tasks that we identify in an effort to improve his own self-determination. I informed Eric early in our relationship that he and only he can be the determining factor in applying to and eventually being accepted into graduate school. Similar to what my brother taught me about always being prepared, I imparted that wisdom to Eric for the sole purpose of enhancing his self-determination. By this means, my mentoring of Kujichagulia allowed Eric to be effective with his follow-through and consistency. In this way, Eric easily benefited from my R.A.M.-focused mentoring because he allowed himself to become more self-determined—enhancing Eric's desire to pursue his doctoral degree.

Sherrie's Succeeding Trust

One significant mentoring relationship that I established over the past five years is with a client and his caregiver, Peter and Sherrie, who reside in the Bayview Hunters Point area of San Francisco. Within the first six months of meeting Sherrie, we began to trust one another. Sherrie informed me that she was watching me closely when I was first assigned to her son (Peter) as his mentor. After we began to talk more candidly about our shared experiences as African Americans living in San Francisco, I noticed that Sherrie became more comfortable.

Relationship.

The initial phases of my authentic relationship with Sherrie ignited because of the relatable coincidences that Sherrie and I shared. In this case, it was our shared experiences of institutional racism in San Francisco. Because we were able to open up to one another about our stories, we began to believe that we truly valued each other. Truly or authentically believing that another human being cares for you is a characteristic that Nodding (1992) identifies as an essential part of a symbiotic caring relationship.

Even more, as our relationship has improved over the years, I have been able to work with Sherrie on strengthening her parenting skills, professional development and academic skills. Because of my authentic R.A.M. relationship, Sherrie disclosed that she appreciated my ability to relate with her in a nonjudgmental way while encouraging both her and her son to achieve their goals.

Accountability.

From the onset of my introduction to Sherrie and Peter, accountability was important and prevalent in their lives. After making several appointments, including school visits and one-on-one mentoring with Peter, I noticed that Sherrie had a gift of being accountable unlike most of the parents I encounter. In fact, Sherrie had even asked me on a number of occasions how she could improve her accountability. I was bewildered yet eagerly excited to fulfill Sherrie's request of strengthening her own sense of accountability. Because Sherrie exhibited an existing appreciation for accountability, especially her timeliness and organizational skills, I decided to teach her about being prepared for school meetings. As we met weekly, I encouraged Sherrie to organize her binders for Peter in a way that they spoke to his academic strengths. For example, I instructed her and Peter to maintain a binder full of his homework assignments and report cards. As the months progressed, Sherrie began to create all types of binders and folders that included Peter's important school documents.

Sherrie even arranged a folder and binder of her own important school documents. Sherrie was attending a local junior college. On one particular occasion Sherrie and I were both preparing for Peter's Individual Educational Planning (I.E.P.) meeting at his middle school. As I prepared my notes and made copies of important documents to share with the school support team (SST), Sherrie had already beat me to the point. She had uniquely prepared an agenda and other important documents to share with the SST in an effort to maximize the meeting time for Peter. I congratulated Sherrie for her commitment and accountability to the process of Peter's I.E.P.

Mentoring.

The significant mentoring that took place in my relationship with Sherrie involved my specific advice of binder-organizing and paperwork preparation. More specifically, I observed that as I taught Sherrie how to better organize her binders to support Peter's academic needs, she listened and followed through immediately. This process of immediate follow-through (accountability) is different with every person. Fortunately, Sherrie was often motivated and inspired in my presence. In fact, I have also noticed that Sherrie was full of enthusiasm when we were working on organizational projects. In this way, my mentoring process with Sherrie was stress-free in that Sherrie demonstrated an innate desire to be mentored. For instance, when we would conduct our weekly mentoring sessions, Sherrie was always prepared and approached all of my homework assignments (i.e., binder management tasks) with excitement. Sherrie disclosed to me often that I made her excited just by my mere presence. When I asked Sherrie to elaborate, she informed "...I wanna do better around you Dr. Horn... you make me wanna be a better person... You don't judge me..." (Researcher Journal, 2015).

Jordan's Eagerness

I clearly remember my R.A.M. engagement with Jordan, which occurred about three years ago. Jordan was an African American elementary school mentee referred to me for general guidance and support. As I walked into Jordan's home for the first time, I observed that he had a smile that lit up the entire room. Jordan was around eight years old and was eagerly awaiting my arrival. With hasty determination, Jordan oriented me to the house, swiftly running into his room to obtain his school supplies.

Relationship.

Jordan resembled an eager child on the first day of school. As we began our introductions, I noticed that he was overly excited. He often interrupted my legalese explanation of the purpose of mentoring, which included explaining the totality of my services. Jordan had no patience with explanations and parameters; he was on board with Dr. Horn's R.A.M. Hence, Jordan and I embarked on a year-long R.A.M. engagement. Jordan and I formed our relationship through our similar backgrounds and excitement for the outdoors. Using my Umoja spirit of unity, I engaged with Jordan through our shared passion for hiking and going to the beach. As a result, Jordan and I were able to foster a relationship almost immediately.

Unlike the hesitancy and reluctance from many of my Black male mentees exposed to trauma, Jordan dove into our R.A.M. relationship with enthusiasm. Jordan was born and raised in the Bay Area and was currently living in San Francisco when we first met. At an early age, Jordan had been exposed to domestic violence, witnessing his mother being verbally and physically abused by his biological father. After many court appearances and removals from his home, Jordan was finally stabilized with his mother.

Jordan and I were as thick as thieves. We played outside at the local park frequently and attended movies together. I remember ringing the doorbell one evening to pick Jordan up for a night out on the town. As I waited for Jordan to come to the door, I heard the hustle and bustle of footsteps until Jordan finally emerged at the door. Later, his mom confided in me that on the nights that Jordan knew I was taking him out, after hearing the doorbell, he would nearly knock down his brothers and sisters until he reached the front door. Hence, my R.A.M. consistency and ability to show up motivated Jordan.

During our outings, Jordan and I often talked about being happy. He disclosed that he enjoyed spending time with me because of my playful spirit, especially the way I played with him at the beach and the park. When Jordan and I were together, we played as if we had no cares or responsibilities in the world. As I reflected on my 12 months of engagement with Jordan, R.A.M. made Jordan unequivocally happy.

Accountability.

One of the most important concepts of an Ujima spirit (accountability) is listening and following directions. As we met over the first six months, Jordan and I completed homework. Jordan's mother, Ms. Wade, informed me that completing homework was nearly impossible before Jordan met me. When I asked about some of the reasons for his newly found passion for completing school assignments, she discussed my ability to show-up consistently on a weekly basis as the most influential factor in Jordan's homework completion improvement. Ms. Wade would often say to me, "...He (Jordan) never has this type of consistency Dr. Horn...Only his teachers and you..." (Researcher Journal, 2013).

Mentoring.

Using Nia (purpose) with Jordan enabled him to increase his self-esteem and confidence with peer and sibling relationships. When I first met Jordan, his mother and aunt had informed me that he had strained relationships with his siblings due to multiple foster care placements. These placements often separated him from his siblings, inhibiting them from developing healthy sibling relationships, which are crucial to his development. During my engagement, Jordan and his siblings had reunited with their mom—Ms. Wade. On more than one occasion, Jordan and his siblings would argue in my presence. After these arguments occurred, I would talk with Jordan about his involvement to allow him to express his innermost feelings.

After talking with Jordan, I noticed a change in his feelings and behavior with his siblings in subsequent interactions. One of the reasons Jordan began improving his interactions with his siblings was due to my mentoring how to engage in healthy dialogue. For example, as part of our engagement, I would often role model Jordan's siblings using typical subjects of contention. In this way, Jordan was able to practice experiencing stress-inducing dialogues about which we were able to dissect and debrief afterwards. When Jordan's mom asked me about these activities, she would explain that she could also see a change in Jordan's relationship with his siblings, especially his younger sister.

Most significantly, I would also discuss with Jordan the purpose of being an older brother, describing his responsibility of being a protector and teacher. Jordan looked at me with reverence as I discussed "Big Brother" responsibilities. Jordan's mom often credited my mentoring by stating, "Dr. Horn...you his mentor...you be teaching him things his father never taught him." (Researcher Journal, 2013). My Nia mentoring inevitably helped Jordan to become more positive in his interactions with his younger sister. Similar to the "father-like" care described in Horn (2010), my Nia spirit helped to improve Jordan's sibling relationships.

The above portraits of engagement briefly describe how I have used R.A.M. to inspire, encourage and motivate human beings. In chapter 4, I describe how a long-term mentoring relationship has allowed one individual to become my most inspired mentee. In this next example, R.A.M. inspires a mentee to reach a new level of personal and professional achievement.

Reflection Questions for Chapter 3

1. Everyone experiences transitions in life. What type of transitions do your students, clients, or colleagues face and how might you use a R.A.M. approach to support their successful progress?

2. How might you use a R.A.M. approach to help students, clients, or colleagues identify short-term objectives that will lead them toward their longer term goals?

3. What elements of R.A.M. reinforce consistency in striving toward long-term goals?

4. As illustrated in these portraits, enthusiasm for learning and growing is a key factor for successful development. In what ways can R.A.M. foster enthusiasm in students, clients, or colleagues?

5. Consider your previous answers. What specific steps can you take with your students, clients, or colleagues to support their transitions, focus them on meaningful, long-term goals, maintain consistency, and promote enthusiasm?

CHAPTER 4

LAWRENCE'S INFLUENCE ON MY WORK

What more can I say about Lawrence Reese except for the undisputed fact that he is on fire! Lawrence is a mentee whom I have taught, counseled and coached for over five years. After being burned over 90% of his body in a motorcycle accident, Lawrence fought his way back from being an invalid to becoming a scholar in the field of disability studies. To gain his goal, Lawrence used R.A.M. to empower himself into a confident, strong, Black, professional male.

I've known Lawrence all of my life. Lawrence has been a part of my family since I was born. He was good friends with my first cousins and uncles on my father's side of our family. We actually met face-to-face 20 years ago when we both attended City College of San Francisco (CCSF). I was a rambunctious, testosterone-driven football player, and Lawrence was one of California's leading track and field athletes. When I reflect upon our years at CCSF as zealous college students, I visualize Lawrence's smile. He has a charismatic smile that makes you feel like you are the only person in a room.

As a student, Lawrence confided in me that he was not as serious and focused as most CCSF students. He often partied, drank and rode his motorcycle as his main form of respite. After his track and field career ended, Lawrence would often ride his motorcycle around the city for fun. After his accident, Lawrence stated that he felt that his life was over. With the aid of his number one support system, his mother, and some audacious doctors and nurses, Lawrence made a partial recovery.

After his physical recovery, Lawrence began his journey to mental fulfillment, returning to CCSF as a student and eventually becoming a full-time employee. Lawrence's journey back to becoming mentally capable was just beginning. Lawrence disclosed to me in many individual coaching sessions that his so-called friends, colleagues and supervisors were treating him with little to no respect. Teachers did not have patience for his mental limitations and many of his colleagues looked down upon him. Unbeknownst to them, Lawrence had suffered trauma to his brain because of his horrific motorcycle accident.

As the years evolved at CCSF, Lawrence became frustrated and unmotivated until he finally had had enough. One sunny afternoon at a local coffee shop in San Francisco, Lawrence and I met face-to-face yet again. Immediately, Lawrence used his radiant smile to beckon me over to his table. After talking with me about his academic struggles at CCSF, I gave my sworn word of honor that I would mentor Lawrence to help him regain his confidence as a student—the same confidence he revealed as California's top track and field athlete.

After a couple of months of cat and mouse (i.e., missed phone calls, unresponsive emails and cancelled appointments), Lawrence and I began a mentor-mentee relationship that would develop into one of my most meaningful one-on-one engagements of R.A.M. in my 20 years of teaching, counseling and coaching. In the beginning of our R.A.M. engagement sessions, I set the boundaries for Lawrence, including (1) my assessment and evaluation as a coach, (2) our weekly meetings, which eventually moved to monthly, and (3) his use of the H.A.I. as his primary tool for changing his life.

Relationship

A few weeks into our weekly R.A.M. sessions, Lawrence was taking hold of the R.A.M. tenets, particularly his ability to remain accountable to this process. As Lawrence developed into a leading student, mentee and advisee, I observed that he possessed three distinct skills to make him a successful R.A.M. candidate.   First, he demonstrated a comprehensive knowledge of underserved families. Second, he had significant leadership skills among his colleagues at CCSF.   Third, he was capable of empowering other disabled individuals through his strength and resiliency spirit. These three skills link directly to the elements of R.A.M.

Using a spirit of Nia (purpose), Lawrence and I connected on our shared purpose of serving impoverished families. Lawrence and I would often discuss how to improve underserved communities of color by hypothesizing action-oriented agendas that would address their needs. In many of our early interactions, we genuinely discussed how to improve the plight of Black America. Our relationship was thus formed from our shared purpose of serving others. As we formed and strengthened our relationship, Lawrence began improving his mentor-mentee relationships with student-athletes at the computer lab where he worked as an academic coach.

For example, as we began discussing the importance of our relationship in Lawrence's life, namely the way I encouraged and validated him, Lawrence informed me that he began fostering similar Nia (purpose) relationships with student-athletes in his computer lab. Lawrence described that he began encouraging the athletes to look beyond playing junior college football because this life often can be short-lived. As a result of his mentoring skills, Lawrence described that many of these students approached him after the end of their careers as athletes at CCSF, thanking him for his advice. In this way, my purpose-driven (Nia) relationship with Lawrence inspired him to transfer the spirit of Nia, including being encouraging and validating, to the student-athletes he serves—many of whom are extremely impoverished.

As a result of Lawrence's relationship-building skills, I have been able to witness firsthand the positive impact of his cultural awareness on hundreds of CCSF athletes. For example, Lawrence serves as a model for younger colleagues' behavior in the field of mentoring at CCSF. He is an exceptional organizational leader and has been pivotal in enhancing the curriculum and administration policies at the CCSF student-athlete computer lab through his culturally aware consultation and advice. Many student-athletes have benefited from Lawrence's advice because they are able to make the necessary adjustments to their class schedules, taking courses that will allow them into four year universities regardless of football responsibilities. Thus, his consultations have had direct impact on improving how CCSF staff and administrators view diversity among their athletes.

Accountability

As our relationship strengthened throughout the years, I began to teach Lawrence skills of accountability that would guide him as he developed into a more confident student. One of my first lessons to impart with Lawrence was the ability and courage to place boundaries with friends, family members and colleagues. Placing boundaries allows us to withhold or to forgo a task that would limit or hinder our ability to take care of ourselves. In essence, placing boundaries requires us to say (1) yes, (2) maybe or (3) no to people in order to maintain our relationships and accountability.

I noticed that Lawrence said "yes" to almost everyone in his life when we first met, except to himself and his personal needs. In order to limit Lawrence's willingness to say "yes" to everyone, we had to first establish the understanding of why he desired to please everyone, especially his family. In order to break apart his "yes" syndrome, I observed that Lawrence had an uncanny ability to schedule excessive events with family, friends and others before addressing his own needs. This "putting everyone else before himself" limited Lawrence's achievement of his professional and personal goals. Hence, Lawrence allowed for the needs of others to supersede his own professional growth and development.

Through trials and tribulations, Lawrence learned how to place boundaries on his life by gently informing people that his priorities became first and foremost in his life, making him more responsible (Ujima) to his personal and academic life. As I watched him grow and develop into a gentle yet firm soul, Lawrence was able to maximize his study time at CCSF by placing the needs of others second to his own. As a result, he was able to develop a well-designed study plan that included at least four to five hours a day of focused, uninterrupted study.

As our relationship grew more profound, Lawrence embodied an Ujima spirit of responsibility. Simply put, he put himself first (e.g., his studies at CCSF, his health and his employment). Most noteworthy, Lawrence began bourgeoning into an enthusiastic academic junior college scholar—the same eagerness that motivated him 20 years earlier. I labeled Lawrence's newly found motivation as "Lawrence being on fire!" After six months of individual coaching, Lawrence digested the accountability skills (i.e., boundaries and putting self first) in their entirety. He began to strategically plan his personal and professional events within his calendar. He learned to maximize his 168-hour calendar week (see Horn, 2010, for further explanation of maximizing the "168-hour calendar week" concept).

Lawrence was no longer a shy, disabled motorcycle accident victim. He had developed into a young scholar who prepared, studied and practiced every week to seek the maximum benefit from his junior college scholastic studies. Simply put, Lawrence would often say, "I got it!" His understanding and implementation of R.A.M allowed him to become focused on only one identified goal—becoming the most motivated and high-performing CCSF student scholar.

Recently, Lawrence reached the pinnacle of our one-on-one coaching relationship. He has internalized his highly positive self-esteem. This concept is one of the most significant, unintended consequences of R.A.M. After developing authentic caring relationships with individuals, I gradually hold them accountable to achieve their goals through check-ins and consistent positive affirmations. As a result, many individuals whom I teach, counsel and coach often disclose that they "feel better" after they leave my presence. It is this "feeling better" state of being, where I observe the most significant changes in the lives of my students, clients and mentees.

Mentoring

As Lawrence and I forged an unbreakable relationship filled with Nia (purpose), Ujima (responsibility) and Imani (faith), I mentored Lawrence into another level of our R.A.M. relationship— mentoring. My mentoring of Lawrence was founded in the African spirit of Umoja (unity). As Lawrence improved in his mentoring ability and responsibility to himself, I used a spirit of Umoja to work side-by-side with Lawrence in many aspects of his personal and professional development.

Similar to Jordan, I found that Lawrence struggled with his peer relationships at CCSF. As mentioned earlier, many of Lawrence's colleagues and other CCSF staff both intentionally and unintentionally offended Lawrence because of their lack of understanding about the negative impact of Lawrence's Traumatic Brain Injury (TBI). During my engagement, Lawrence often discussed how some staff at CCSF would disrespect him, including professors not making quality time to understand his academic needs, which were confounded with his TBI. As a strategy to improve these tense relationships, I would often talk with Lawrence about his participation in an effort to allow him to express his deepest feelings.

After engaging in these debriefing discussions or check-ins with Lawrence, I noticed a change in his moods and actions with his colleagues in subsequent engagements. Akin to improving Jordan's relationships with his siblings, I used role modeling with Lawrence. As Lawrence and I met weekly, I would role model a typical combative conversation that occurred between Lawrence and a CCSF colleague. After practicing several ways to converse using positive language, Lawrence was able to practice stress-inducing discourses (i.e., stressful vignettes), which we were then able to examine. Lawrence would often thank me, saying "Man...thank you for helping me improve my communication skills... I can see it's working...I'm using it man... I'm really using it..." (Researcher Journal, 2013). Hence, I used my Nia spirit of mentoring to improve Lawrence's sense of purpose amongst his colleagues at CCSF.

As a reminder, Lawrence disclosed that in addition to our R.A.M. relationship, life experience and community resources aided in his "getting it!" Throughout many of our candid conversations, Lawrence disclosed that life experience had assisted in his R.A.M. transformation. For instance, Lawrence disclosed that because of his age and his "no bullshit" (i.e., serious outlook on life) temperament on life that he has been able to absorb some of his most memorable life teachings, including R.A.M. Lawrence describes, "Man...it's easy because of my age...I'm older so I can internalize the process more…I'm serious about my education and my life…" (Researcher Journal, 2015).

Lawrence elaborated by describing his recent task-oriented study and work schedule. Lawrence explains, "…I'm serious Aaron…I wake up, eat, pray, workout and study…That's my schedule….I go to work and then I get my butt in bed!" (Researcher Journal, 2015). Lawrence explained to me that he is regimented in his schedule because he feels that he does not have time to waste, unlike many younger people who may be living a haphazard lifestyle due to their youth. On the contrary, Lawrence believes that "Father Time" is scrutinizing his every step of existence.

Similarly, Lawrence also revealed that community resources play a big role in his success as a current California State college student. Lawrence reminded me that as he began to regain his confidence in college he increased his involvement in the disability community, especially accessing services at the local city level, City College and State College. Lawrence added, "As I started to access these resources…I felt empowered to do better…It was like they (i.e., the various disability resources) added to my accountability…" (Researcher Journal, 2015). In essence, Lawrence believed that accessing disability resources, he was empowered to complete the academic rigor, which made him more accountable to our R.A.M. relationship—enhancing his academic accountability. Lawrence described the significance with this connection and access to disability resources as the link that made him more serious about his education. In his words, "It's hard to explain… I just became more accountable." (Researcher Journal, 2015).

Through his weekly diligent listening and questioning, Lawrence's implementation of R.A.M. yielded astounding results. Over the course of our five-year, one-on-one coaching relationship, Lawrence has been able to (1) increase his personal study efforts, (2) become more confident about his academic proficiency, (3) make better choices regarding healthy relationships, (4) improve his fondness for reading, (5) strengthen his organizational skills, (6) improve his communication skills, and (7) increase his overall CCSF grade point average.

Lawrence's success with R.A.M. fuels my passion to help the plight of adolescent Black males who struggle with mental illness, disability issues, and detention within the systems of special education, juvenile hall, or prison. I dedicate my heart to these Black males! Additionally, Lawrence's success has further prompted my passion for maximizing my relationships by serving other Black males who struggle. After reflecting upon Lawrence's life, I thought about my passion and the reasons why I believe so strongly in the plight of Black males.

I have always been passionate for young Black males. My passion is rooted in my childhood being raised a strong Black male. Because of our racialized history in this country, I am focused on promoting education for Black males while helping them to develop effective coping mechanisms for surviving mainstream America. In addition, I have worked in almost every capacity regarding the plight of Black males, including being a teacher, counselor and coach. My mission to help the plight of Black males is thoroughly documented with professional employment in this particular field. My passion for helping Black males is rooted in my lived experiences as a Black male in white America.

When I was growing up in the Bay Area, I attended public and private schools. Within these schools, I felt isolated because of my skin color, my culture, and the lack of people in these schools who looked like me. After becoming a young adult, adolescent Black males expressed similar feelings to me. Most poignant, as I began my career in the field of human service, I started to feel good addressing the plight of adolescent Black males. Although this "feeling good" was egocentric, I just remembered feeling good all of the time. When I began my career in the group home system as a residential counselor, I remember having a myriad of feelings after completing my shift. The work as a residential counselor was exhausting, but I loved working with adolescent Black males.

I also remember when I first became a licensed teacher and began working in the public schools. To witness the smiles on the faces of adolescent Black males as I walked down the hallways was invaluable. On the other hand, these adolescent Black males often had faces filled with despair and deep-rooted anger—anger I was very familiar with. In spite of the rage and unhappiness on their faces, I was so enthralled to be teaching all of these adolescent Back males. As Lawrence's story of success resonates within me, it reminds me that my reason for working with Black males has more to do with me feeling great about giving my service to this population. I dedicate my heart to all of the Black males in America—wherever they are and amid all of their struggles.

Overall, Lawrence's application of R.A.M. allowed him to develop into an academic powerhouse, researching and presenting on newly developed trends in the disabled community. Since Lawrence's "on fire" presence, I have also observed a noticeable difference in his academic rigor. Five years ago, Lawrence fretted about taking more than two classes per semester. Now, Lawrence becomes eager for the opportunity of taking three or more classes. Reaffirming his excitement, Lawrence often repeats in his raspy voice, "I got it!" In return, Lawrence has refueled my passion for teaching, counseling and coaching Black males to achieve their personal and professional goals of success.

Reflection Questions for Chapter 4

1. What are some of the personal struggles of your students, clients, or colleagues (e.g., poverty, abuse, institutional racism, etc.)?

2. How can you use R.A.M. to address some of their personal struggles?

3. What are some of the academic/cognitive/organizational struggles of your students, clients, or colleagues (e.g., reading, time management, etc.)?

4. How can you use R.A.M. to address some of these academic and professional struggles?

5. What specific resources or strategies can you share to address these personal and academic challenges?

6. How are the special needs (e.g., people with learning difficulties, emotional or behavioral and physical limitations) of your students, clients, or colleagues addressed in your setting?

7. How can you use R.A.M. your setting to address these special needs?

8. Think of one particular individual and develop an action plan of specific steps that you can take to support that person's personal growth and development.

CHAPTER 5

THE SECRET FORMULA FOR R.A.M. SUCCESS

In order for R.A.M. to develop and grow in the way that I have practiced it over my 20 years as a professional in the human service field, there is a non-linear formula that R.A.M. practitioners should consider while nurturing their own R.A.M. relationships. The three ingredients for a true R.A.M. relationship include (1) being nonjudgmental, (2) having patience with the process of R.A.M. and (3) being open to the unexpected.

Being Nonjudgmental

Many of my family members, clients and colleagues have always stated that I have been nonjudgmental. For me, I have not practiced being nonjudgmental because it has been a part of my personality since I can remember. I define nonjudgmental as being open and accepting to everyone and everybody, regardless of their belief systems or cultural practices. The most successful R.A.M. relationships have materialized out of my ability to be nonjudgmental. For instance, I was working with a young African American male client who claimed he was hearing voices from his grandmother who had passed away when he was younger. As he described these voices, it was evident that he was tentative in his disclosure about such personal experiences, especially because of the connection to what the American Psychiatric Association (2013) identifies as being related to Schizophrenia.

On the contrary, many cultures claim to hear voices from their ancestors and engage in personal conversations, especially African American cultures. Afraid of being diagnosed as a schizophrenic, many people of color, including me, refrain from discussing that they speak with their deceased relatives. Similarly, my client's hesitancy had kept him isolated from his peers and relatives. After assessing that he did not meet the criteria of Schizophrenia including the subtypes (catatonic, disorganized and paranoid), we began on the journey of discussing the positive outcomes of speaking with his ancestors (Williams, 2008). In the months to follow, my client began trusting me more and we began embarking in a therapeutic alliance that set the stage for my client's eventual healing pertaining to his grandmother's death and its relevance to his current life. My client would later disclose to me in subsequent sessions that he appreciated my ability to be understanding and nonjudgmental about his report of hearing his grandmother speak to him. My ability to be nonjudgmental has always helped me to understand the diverse perspectives of everyone I encounter, particularly as a therapist.

Having Patience with the Process of R.A.M.

I admit, I have not always been a patient person. It took me many years to develop patience because I realized that patience, akin to the process of R.A.M., is an ongoing life-long process of development. Similarly, in order to foster an authentic R.A.M. relationship, you have to be patient with its process. As mentioned earlier, R.A.M. is a multifaceted process that encompasses various aspects—namely Afrocentric principles of the Nguzo Saba. When engaging in the process of R.A.M., it's important to remember that everyone engages in relationships differently. Because of an individual's intersectionality differences (e.g., race, culture, gender, sexual identity, etc.), R.A.M. does not occur instantaneously.

One of the components of R.A.M. is trust and trust can take years to develop depending on the people engaged in the relationship, especially in the cases of therapist-client, teacher-student and mentor-mentee. Case in point, several years ago as a mentor I was working with a young African American client named Peter, mentioned in Chapter 3, who was exposed to trauma. Like many individuals exposed to trauma, Peter shunned relationships and often isolated himself. Growing up in one of San Francisco's violent neighborhoods, Peter had experienced domestic violence and had been shot in the stomach. Due to the multiple internal and external processes caused by trauma (Boyd-Franklin, 2003; Horn, 2013), Peter did not trust other people, understandably so. As I began working with Peter, using R.A.M. as the foundation, Peter slowly and cautiously trusted me more. One day, Peter and I were walking in a local neighborhood park discussing his progress in school. As we walked along the path, Peter gently reached up and grabbed my hand for comfort. Although I had experienced this physical sign of trust from other clients, I was amazed because I had no idea Peter had developed trust in me so rapidly.

As we finished our walk, I remember speaking with his mother about this rapid expression of trust. Peter's mother responded in a matter-of-fact way, "...Of course Dr. Horn...Peter really like you...It took him a long time...It's something about your presence....He just trust you..." (Researcher Journal, 2013). From the onset of our relationship until the moment Peter had reached for my hand had been about a year. Although there is no time frame regarding how individuals trust, Peter's trust had stunned me because I expected years of ambivalence and resistance before Peter showed any signs of trust. The message of this lesson was that R.A.M., just like any other process, takes patience.

Being Open to the Unexpected

Being open to the unexpected is a huge ingredient for successful R.A.M. Simply put, do not try to control the process or force the outcomes of your R.A.M. relationships. As mentioned above and throughout this book, R.A.M. is an intricate process with many aspects. The basic purpose of R.A.M. is to deepen your relationship with another human being. The unanticipated consequences of R.A.M. could include many things, including (1) improved student behavior, (2) a more trustworthy therapeutic alliance between a therapist and their client and (3) improved healthcare for a patient.

In fact, I have experienced all three of the above-mentioned. One of the most memorable unexpected R.A.M. outcomes occurred between myself and my nutritionist Gary at the Veterans Hospital (VA). Gary is a young slender-built Asian American who has been working at a local Bay Area VA for several years. What stood out about Gary when I first met him was his taut posture and attention to details, namely his patient's needs. I was referred to Gary for weight management issues. I had been struggling for unknown reasons to manage my weight. Almost immediately, Gary used a R.A.M. style of engagement to better understand me as a person and a patient.

After getting to know Gary for several months, I appreciated his bedside manner, especially his purpose-driven style of nutritional care. Gary would always start and begin his sessions with a check-in relating to the fact that he wanted to make me feel better and healthier. This was the overall goal of Gary's nutritional message. Next, he gradually asked about my current mental health struggles that were directly and indirectly related to my weight management and then he strategically used nutritional education to enhance my knowledge of nutrition and how I could improve my nutritional habits. Although Gary was able to improve my knowledge of nutrition with his caregiving R.A.M., one of the unexpected outcomes was a decrease in my nutritional intake during my intense cardiovascular activities.

In one of Gary's nutrition sessions, he informed me that most professional athletes take in about 3,000 to 5,000 calories per day during their training. Little did Gary know, I was taking in almost double—at least 6,000 to 10,000. After I informed Gary of my intake and sudden decrease, he congratulated me on my reduction. Although I was burning an enormous amount of calories on my 30-mile hikes in one day, Gary reminded me that I did not need 6,000 to 10,000 calories to replenish myself unless I was going to become a professional long distance hiker. Gary stated, "That's a lot of calories...I think Michael Phelps takes in about 12,000 calories per day when he is in training….But he burns that off quickly…" (Researcher Journal, 2013).

I am by far no Michael Phelps and nor do I want to be him. Because I love my regimented hiking, I was able to internalize Gary's nutritional message that calorie intake affects our weight. When I first signed up for Gary's sessions, I had no idea that I would decrease my calorie intake, one of the main reasons my weight had ballooned. I don't know if Gary had a reduction of calories in mind, but the unexpected outcome was just that—my calorie reduction led to weight loss. In this case, Gary's purpose-driven R.A.M. (i.e., Nia [purpose]) led to an unexpected outcome of calorie reduction.

When R.A.M. Does Not Exist

When R.A.M. is not in existence, there can be detrimental aspects. For example, I usually wash my car in a local Bay Area car wash every so often. Last year, a manager at this car wash literally screamed at me after I tried to resolve a problem about one of their services. Long story short, as I was leaving and saying to the cashier "well....this is my final time here..." She said, "No....don't leave us.... we really had a crazy day today...someone just yelled at our manager before you came in...." I immediately whispered to myself, ""hum...interesting..." Shortly after the incident took place, the manager came back in and said, "I'm sorry...I apologize...here is a free car wash...I misunderstood your complaint." (Researcher Journal, 2015).

I then abruptly interrupted and said, "...I understand but this is my last day here...I do not want your free car wash and I do not appreciate you yelling at me and slamming your hands on top of the table... I have been coming here for more than five years and I have never been disrespected the way you responded to me today at this establishment..." (Researcher Journal, 2015).

As he attempted to apologize more, I ignored him and continued my conversation with the cashier, said goodbye, got in my truck and drove off. This story is important in that I have reflected that when R.A.M. is not present, devastating human events can occur. In this case, there was a lack of understanding on part of both offended parties—the car wash manager and me. In addition, the lack of R.A.M. among human beings caused me to reflect upon my personal growth and development as it pertains to the human development journey in the following manner:

(1) I am constantly developing as a human being. This means that I need to continue to understand that every human being has a history and a context that impacts their human development.

(2) I need to learn that at every minute, human development is occurring. Human development is fluid not static. The manager of this car wash was impacted by someone else's anger; thus, his unresolved anger was transferred onto the next customer. Namely, me.

(3) Although human development is fluid. I need to maintain safe and appropriate boundaries in order to protect myself by establishing "limits" as to how much of "other people's stuff" I can

hold on a daily basis. By this means, I am a "container" for my clients, which can impact my understanding of others after I leave my job. For instance, when I pulled into the car wash, I was already "wound up" from holding stuff in—my shoulders were rock hard from stress. This stress inevitably played a part into my reaction to the car wash manager who was wound up from someone else's anger placed onto him.

I say all of that to say that I am still learning and what I do know is that I need to continue to practice R.A.M. with everyone I engage with, especially those I encounter consistently. In the case of the incident with the manager of the car wash, R.A.M. could have prevented our disconnection.

Reflection Questions for Chapter 5

1.   What strategies might you employ to decrease tendencies to judge those around you—your students, clients, colleagues, friends, and family? Can you stop and reconsider a judgmental comment before you utter it?

2.   How do you practice patience with those around you? What types of strategies might help you wait for outcomes to occur without forcing them?

3.   Have you experienced situations in which an unexpected benefit occurred? Can you think of times when your inability to remain open to unanticipated consequences resulted in a missed opportunity to learn, grow, or help others?

4.   How can you apply the secret formula for R.A.M. success to challenges that you face?

5.   How can you help those around you apply the secret formula for R.A.M. success to challenges that they face?

CHAPTER 6

CONCLUSION

In this chapter, I leave the reader with final thoughts about the significance of R.A.M. As discussed in previous chapters, I hope the reader has gained a better understanding of R.A.M. and how it has benefited not only the lives that I have engaged with over my 20 year career but also my life.

My Passion for Creating R.A.M.

As in my previous books, I need to first elucidate that R.A.M. is not a "one size fits all" strategy. It was a strategy birthed within me through the Horn and Reynolds bloodline of my mother, grandmother and older brother and in the long run improved by the United States Army. In essence, R.A.M. is a way of life that has enabled Dr. Horn to be successful as a teacher, counselor and coach. R.A.M. can be very impactful but should not be used to "solve" or "fix" a specific problem. It is one approach to deepening human connections.

I believe the most noteworthy element about my concept of R.A.M. is that it cannot be practiced unless it is authentic. Because it was birthed in me through my genealogy, R.A.M. has no superficial roots. It is a concept foreign to today's world of being "friended" or "unfriended." R.A.M. is a theme that only the greatest communicators and relationship experts dare to pontificate about. R.A.M. can only be practiced when a person's heart is pure. By this means, when a human being is genuinely engaged with another human being for the sole purpose of making that person feel better, then, and only then, can R.A.M. can be employed as a means to deepen the connection between two authentically caring individuals.

My passion for developing R.A.M. into a methodology stems from my 20 years of successful teaching, counseling and coaching of Black males (see Horn, 2010). Moreover, the recent "slaughtering" of Black males has significantly increased my passion for employing

R.A.M. into their lives. For example, I have enveloped myself within a whirlwind of emotions given the recent and ongoing slayings of young Black males across America, beginning with the unnecessary and unprovoked deaths of Trayvon Martin and Oscar Grant.

After countless hours of reflecting on their deaths, I can remember having tears in my eyes as I watched listlessly to the news recounting their stories. The tragic deaths of Black males have always baffled me, even before these recent events and my creation of R.A.M. I have always been troubled at the countless Black men who were discarded like trash during slavery. It begs the recent trending and hashtag question which I have come to reflect on almost daily—Do Black lives matter?

For myself, it's an obvious Yes, but for others, I cannot safely nor sanely answer that question. What about the thousands of young Black males with whom I have worked over my career? I just couldn't seem to get over how many young Black males die pointlessly at the hands of policemen or wannabe neighborhood watchmen. The pointless killings of young Black males have, in fact, become normalized. At one point in my recent reflections, I noticed that I began questioning my work. I asked myself, "am I doing enough…Is my professional career helping these young Black males in the way they need to be helped?" It was after these reflections, that I began working even more arduously on how to expound upon and institutionalize my concept of R.A.M.

It is important to note that the intention of my aforementioned reflections is not to demonize white Americans or segregate murder by class. All senseless killings are wrong, no matter whom the perpetrator and victims are. In fact, most killings involve people of the same race. Killings by police and vigilantes to all Americans are egregious. It is my hope that R.A.M. can be used in future training of police cadets or in the retraining of police officers to lessen the unnecessary killings of unarmed civilians.

Although R.A.M. has been used to cultivate fantastic friendships with all races, I use it specifically to teach, counsel and coach young Black males. For these reasons, I yearn to have my concept of R.A.M. adopted by young Black males across America as a part of their individual culture and legacy. My hope and desire is that R.A.M. will inspire a generation of young Black males to continue their work of improving the future of Black America.

R.A.M. Changed Me Forever

R.A.M. has changed me forever. In particular, R.A.M. has brought me to a place in my life where I remain focused. For the past two years and most recently, I have been focusing on (1) completing my hours for my marriage and family therapist licensure—hours have been obtained, (2) becoming vulnerable and falling in love—currently in love, and (3) building my thriving business of Horn Development Consulting—currently building my business. Toward success with these achievements and many more, R.A.M. keeps me focused.

The main reason why my consulting business is thriving is because I stopped interacting and connecting with others who do not possess a similar spirit of R.A.M. Therefore, after I realized how R.A.M. kept me in the circle of success, especially when I congregated with other R.A.M. believers, I began increasing my social network of R.A.M. associates. As a result, I began an ongoing, reciprocal process of R.A.M. mentoring in which people whom I am mentoring and vice versa are becoming successful at completing their personal and professional goals. R.A.M. has changed my life forever.

Most important to my success and the process of R.A.M. is my relationship with God. After meditating, praying, reflecting and reading God's word, I have been able to achieve some of the most monumental milestones in my life, including my successful completion of my five year Army career, my doctorate degree, my research publications and my relationship with Colette. I will continue down the path of "keeping God first" while demonstrating a spirit of R.A.M. because it has permitted me to achieve all of my goals thus far.

My Passion for Teaching R.A.M.

My passion for teaching R.A.M. at the university level has always been fueled by my personal practice as an educator and advocate for disenfranchised families. I have committed my life to serving underserved populations throughout the Greater Bay Area and beyond. Therefore, I firmly believe that my teaching and practice have comingled to create a hybrid graduate curriculum that challenges the norms and beliefs of the students I encounter.

In various presentations, lectures and seminars I employ my unique engagement style of R.A.M. to create a classroom environment that allows students to feel empowered while discussing the most critical subjects in the field of education and counseling. I incorporate into my lectures components of intersectionality (e.g., race, sexuality, gender, socio-economic status, etc.) and how they influence perspective and engagement style with clients and their families. In essence, I promote a safe and challenging academic environment where students can present their life story along with the stories of their clients and families whom they serve.

My approach to teaching R.A.M., particularly related to community mental health, is infused with my professional expertise and training with children and adolescents. Along with my theoretical belief systems of how to critically assess the structural factors that impact the lives of underserved families, students work individually and in groups to complete projects that encompass these concepts. I use a dialogical framework with open-ended questions, often leading to inspired students who publish their research, create their own K-University Social Justice curriculum and complete their graduate theses. Many of my students are inspired by my pedagogy, which uses active listening and face-to-face dialogue to engage with their clients and students through clinical and K-12 classroom teaching—improving therapist-client and teacher-student trust. Additionally, students impart components of my university teaching within their clinical and teaching practice to help them understand the importance of helping families find ways to be positive when living amidst persistent disadvantages.

Moreover, I use my teaching of R.A.M. to elucidate the importance of providing mental health services to underserved families, using a social-justice-oriented belief system. By providing students with tangible opportunities to help underserved families from my clinical practice and research, students develop therapeutic skills to improve the resiliency of children and families who endure significant obstacles. Most noteworthy, I use my teaching to test new counseling techniques, specifically culturally relevant modalities, to broaden my perspective and those of my students concerning the trans-generational poverty and trauma of underserved families.

Most importantly, I promote a classroom environment based upon the reciprocal process of R.A.M., where students are encouraged to speak up and speak out about critical concepts of psychology, especially by challenging outdated paradigms of psychological thinkers, researchers and clinicians. This approach includes supporting a classroom environment where mutual trust, respect and dialogue are included in all aspects of my lectures. In particular, my pedagogy is inclusive of the sensitive needs of my students' intersectionality, including able-bodiedness, culture, sexuality, gender and socioeconomic status. Because of my attentiveness to create a safe environment for my class, students feel safe, respected and welcomed. Finally, I thrive to promote a classroom environment that continuously challenges my existing belief systems as well as those of the university, professors and my students themselves. By this means, I uphold R.A.M. throughout all aspects of my life.

In conclusion, my concept of R.A.M. has been used with human beings to enhance life skills, parenting skills, educational goals, family goals, mental health issues and communication skills. R.A.M has changed me forever because it allows me to forge authentic relationships with people through one-on-one, face-to-face, nonjudgmental conversations in an effort to make them feel better about themselves and their lives in general. It is my desire, that you (the reader) utilize my concept of R.A.M. to deepen your connection with the human beings you engage with every day.

Reflection Questions for Chapter 6

1. How do you demonstrate respect for your students, clients, or colleagues?

2. In what ways can R.A.M. be used to demonstrate your respect?

3. Describe how you communicate expectations with students, clients, or colleagues.

4. How can R.A.M. be used to clarify your expectations?

5. How do your students, clients, or colleagues know you believe in their academic, personal, or professional abilities?

6. In what ways can R.A.M. be used to demonstrate your belief in their abilities?

7. How do you reward others for their efforts?

8. Describe how R.A.M. can be used in your setting as a reward for the efforts of others.

REFERENCES

American Psychiatric Association. (2013). Diagnostic and statistical manual of mental disorders (5th ed.). Washington, DC: Author.

Bennett, L. (2003). *Before the Mayflower: A history of Black America* (6th ed.). Chicago, IL: Penguin Books.

Boyd-Franklin, N. (2003). *Black families in therapy: Understanding the African American experience* (2nd ed.). New York, NY: Guilford Press.

Hardy, K. (2012). Healing the hidden wounds of racial trauma. *Journal of Reclaiming Children and Youth, 22*(1), 24-28.

Horn, A. (2010). *The role of father-like care in the education of young Black males.* New York, NY: Edwin Mellen Press.

Horn, A. (2013). *I Got'Cho Back! Improving relationships with young Black males.* Amazon.com

Magee, R. (2015, May 19). How mindfulness can defeat racial bias. *The Huffington Post.com, Inc.* Retrieved from http://www.huffingtonpost.com.

Noddings, N. (1992). *The challenge to care in schools: An alternative approach to education.* New York, NY: Teachers College Press.

Santrock, J. (2009). *Life-span development.* New York, NY: McGraw-Hill.

Sue, D. W., Capodilupo, C. M., Torino, G. C., Bucceri, J. M., Holder, A. M. B., Nadal, K. L., & Esquilin, M. (2007). Racial microaggressions in everyday life: Implications for clinical practice. *American Psychologist, 62*(4), 271-286.

Williams, C. T. (2008). Paradigm shift in African American funeral customs: Looking through the lens of oral history and consumer culture. *Electronic Theses and Dissertations*. Paper 500.

Wilson, A. (1991). *Understanding Black adolescent male violence: Its remediation and prevention*. New York, NY: Afrikan World InfoSystems.

INDEX

AFTERWORD

In the tradition of my cultural beliefs, I am honored to write an afterword dedicated to those whom I call my extended family. These individuals have played a significant role in my development as an African American male–dedicated to the development of every human being, and particularly young Black males. These individuals fostered the R.A.M. system of deepening human connection, which I have meticulously described in the previous chapters. For these reasons, it is an honor to present the following founding forefathers and foremothers of R.A.M.

First and foremost, thank you Harriet Tubman. You alone helped to free thousands of mentally and spiritually chained African Americans. Your confidence burns fiercely within my spirit.

To Auntie Jeannie, Cousin Demetrius, Cousin Christy and Cousin Talia, thank you for supporting my dreams. Cousin D, I am so proud of your ability to mentor underserved children and families of color.

To Cousin Chris Moore, thank you for always taking care of your cousin when we were growing up. I will never forget our R.A.M. friendship, which was based in solid accountability for one another.

To Uncle Lucias, thank you for your continual teaching, encouragement and prayer. I will always remember to keep God first in my life because of you.

To Cousins Donnell Reynolds, Maylanda Knockum and Daiannie Reynolds, thank you for your love and support. Cousin Donnell, I specifically thank you for your continual R.A.M. monthly check-ins. Your reliability energizes my passion to continue validating R.A.M. on both a national and international level.

To all of my aunts, uncles and cousins on the Horn and Jackson side of the family, I give you a special thank you! To all of you, including Auntie Betty, Uncle Larry, Cousin Lawrence, Cousin

Jazmine, Cousin Marlena, Cousin Etecia, Cousin Nailah, Saffron, Cousin Shawn, Cousin Shawnisha, Cousin Elaina, Cousin Tierra, Uncle Lionel, Cousin Pierre, Uncle Tony, Cousin Miki, Cousin Michelle, Cousin Russell, Uncle Tony, Cousin Anthony, Uncle Lionel, Cousin Naomi, Cousin Nikki, Uncle Roland, Auntie Reggie, Cousin Chris, Cousin Suzy, Uncle Austin, Uncle Wayne, and Uncle Michael. Thank you for always keeping the family together through R.A.M. celebrations.

Auntie Betty, thank you for your continual prayers and support. Your consistent representation of R.A.M. continues to bless our entire family because you fervently believe in the power of prayer.

Cousin Marlena, thank you for demonstrating the spiritual essence of R.A.M. Your genuine care and concern for others, especially underserved girls of color have fueled my passion to further develop R.A.M.

To Cousin Chris Horn, thank you for always being there for me throughout my lifespan development. Your enduring R.A.M. love for family has blessed the entire Horn, Jackson and Reynolds circle.

To Auntie Marva, thank you for supporting my scholastic achievements and for always being a true friend to my mom and our entire family. You are forever interwoven into our entire family network!

To Auntie Shirley, thank you for supporting my writing, travels, teaching and community work with underserved families. You have been the quintessential friend to my mother and I love you for that reason alone.

To my extended mom and little brother Dr. Farris Page and Eric Taylor, thank you both for validating me as a Black man on a daily basis. Our discussions of what it is like to be Black in America have enhanced my mental, physical and spiritual development.

To my best friend, Mr. Robert Lucas and Family (Alana, Brian and David), thank you Rob Luke for modeling R.A.M. through your loyalty. Your profound R.A.M. advice continues to improve my teaching, counseling and coaching of R.A.M.

To Mr. Dave Scott and family, thank you for your committed R.A.M. friendship to my family for over 30 years. Your dependable mentorship to all of the young Black males you teach has allowed me to become an effective R.A.M. teacher, counselor and coach.

To my dear friend and her partner (Soma and Waldemar), thank you Soma for staying connected with our family. Your friendship with my family is a sign of your authentic personalities.

To the Steeno family (Jeff, Connie, Axel, and Chuy), thank you for your tenacious relationship and support. You have always supported me and I will never forget you for the welcoming-R.A.M. spirit that you imparted to me over 10 years ago. Chuy, you are my protector!

To Dr. Lois Merriweather-Moore, thank you for encouraging me to publish my work. You have helped to fuel the institutionalization of R.A.M. through your encouragement.

To my best friend Maurice Lewis, thank you for being another true accountability partner. Our friendship spans over two decades. Your commitment and dedication to the Black community as a Special Education teacher inspires me to continue my work every day!

To my best friend and Fraternity brother (AΦA) Reggie Stewart and family (Lee, Nia, and Noa), thank you for modeling the spirit of R.A.M. in your daily life. I am honored by our life-long R.A.M. relationship.

To my dear friend and Fraternity brother (AΦA) Calvin and your son Darius, thank you for always supporting my academic research and representing R.A.M. through your continual mentoring of your "Father-like Care" spirit that has impacted generations of Black males.

To the most consistent Fraternity brothers of Alpha Phi Alpha (XI Rho Chapter) Larry Goode and AC (Alex Wills), thank you both for always being encouraging and collaborative. When I think about what Alpha means to me, especially XI Rho I always think about AC and Larry. I love you brothers deeply!

To my advisor and Fraternity Brother (ΑΦΑ) Mr. Mauricio Wright, thank you for straightforward-R.A.M. friendship and consultation. You continue to hold me accountable by inspiring me to enhance my clinical and professional skills in the field of counseling.

To my nutritionist, Mr. Gary Yee, thank you for teaching me about calories and nutrition. You're advice has helped me to gain a better understanding on food intake and how that impacts my ability to manage my weight.

To the most prestigious fraternity in the whole wide world, Alpha Phi Alpha Fraternity Incorporated, XI Rho Chapter (Lonnie Holmes, David Angel Harris, Reggie Stewart, Mark Strong, Ngafa Cree, Makail Ali, Sean Clinton, Ricky Robinson, Reggie Parsons, Vester Lee Flanagan, Tony Hazard, Jeffrey Smith, Larry Goode, AC (Alex Wills), Mauricio Wright, Larrel Dean, Osa Bisa, Marcum Jones, Sterling Brown, Asa Randolph, Mychal Lynch, Ajani Byrd, Marcus Logan and many more…), thank you for allowing me to be a part of a lifelong Rites of Passage. Your process has allowed me to become the responsible Black man who is necessary and needed for current and future generations of young Black men in America!

To my best friend of two decades, Delmar Johnson and family (Tracy and Jeaneen). Delmar, thank you for being a R.A.M. accountability partner. Our friendship demonstrates how R.A.M. cultivates and nurtures relationship endurance.

To my dear friend and colleague Mr. Paul Harris of the United States Army. Not only was it a pleasure to serve with you, it has also been a pleasure to be a R.A.M. accountability partner with you. Thank you for taking care of our troops and soldiers! Rangers lead the way!

To my prestigious Black males affiliates of R.A.M., Brad and Onllwyn (Dr. Washington and Dr. Dixon), thank you for always supporting my personal and professional endeavors.

To the Sheppard Family (Edward, Neashelle, and Tiye), thank you for always being in me and for being consistent. You all have benefited me through your R.A.M. spirit of consistency.

Tiye, your uncle is speechless when I think about your achievements. You are nothing less but phenomenal. You continue to inspire and motivate me with your R.A.M. spirit of success.

To my dear brother and sister-in-law, Kenny and Christina, thank you for your consistency and dedicated support. You both embody the spirit of R.A.M. in that you both always achieve your goals because of your ability to deepen your connections with other human beings.

To Kenny, thank you for always being consistent. Our R.A.M. relationship has strengthened me by believing once again that human beings can be consistent with their affection for one another.

To my best friend Mr. Cecil Wong and family, thank you Cecil for demonstrating R.A.M. through your consistency, prayer and faith in God. Your faithful friendship renews my relationship with God.

To my sister and her family (Karla, Alex, and Sebastian), thank you Karla for always including me in your family. It has been nothing but pure joy to watch you emulate R.A.M. through your dependability.

To Belinda Arriaga and family, you are a magnificent illustration of R.AM. Your consistent R.A.M. relationship and prayers have changed my life forever. Thank you for being a practitioner of R.A.M. in both your personal and professional life.

To my dear friend and colleague Ms. Pepper Black, thank you for always supporting my academic endeavors. I look forward to many camping and hiking trips together—sharing nature with our blended families!

To the Psyhogios family (Suzette, Tim, and Ross), thank you for representing R.A.M. throughout your lineage. Ross, I cannot express how I appreciate our R.A.M. relationship. You faithfully continue to represent R.A.M. as a son, attorney, friend, colleague and human being.

To the Griffin family (Byron, Susan, Jeron, and Aislynn), thank you for your persistent friendship and support. You never forget me and I thank you for your genuine R.A.M. relationship.

To Dr. Tyrone Cannon and my USF Gleeson library family (Carmen, Joe Garity, Collette, Matt, Lloyd, Shawn, Sherise, Fabiola, etc.), thank you for allowing me to utilize the library to support my research and passion of sponsoring R.A.M.

To Tyrone, my spiritual father, thank you for being consistent with your guidance, advice and friendship. You continue to illustrate R.A.M. in my life through your fatherly presence.

To the School of Education at the University of San Francisco. Thank you for providing me with two prestigious graduate degrees. A special thanks to Dr. Cori Bussolari, Dr. Mary Coombs, Estella and Donna for your counsel and support as my mentors. You all demonstrate R.A.M. by being such dedicated friends.

To my sister and brother-in-law, Selma Schlesinger and Matt, thank you for family presence in my life. Selma, thank you for crafting such a beautiful portrait that personifies R.A.M. Your R.A.M. relationship personifies the spirit of family.

To my sister Lesley Guth! Thank you for always demonstrating your authentic, genuine and nurturing R.A.M. friendship. Like we always say—friends for life!

To my best friend and R.A.M. accountability partner Eddie Grassi and Shalini, thank you for always being reliable and forthcoming. Your genuine R.A.M. relationship has significantly impacted my life over the past five years.

To Lawrence, the man of the year! You are on fire! Thank you for preserving the tenets of R.A.M. You continue to be a man of accountability and autonomy.

To Eric Taylor, my R.A.M. aficionado. Thank you for demonstrating the achievement spirit of R.A.M. You continue to impress me with your humble spirit. I always Got' Cho Back!

To Shonnie Hardy and Paul, thank you for committing to the genuine relationship and accountability process of R.A.M. You and Paul are forever incorporated as a part of my extended family.

To Mr. Christian Lindner and Ms. Sasha Monteiro, thank you for being my European diplomats of R.A.M. Your consistent communication and check-ins keep me persistently motivated about long-distance R.A.M.

To Pete and Dynamite, two pillars of Bayview Hunters Point, thank you both for representing the Bay View Hunters Point Community for your legacy of consistent R.A.M. for all Black males whom have graced your presence in your esteemed Sportsman Barbershop.

Thank you Mr. and Mrs. Claudius and Jenee Johnson and Khalid. I love you all for modeling the true spirit of the Black family—unconditional and unrelenting love for one another!

Thank you John Marman for two decades of friendship. You are a true master of automobiles and R.A.M. because you demonstrate the humility of God every day. You are always in my prayers.

To my extended family at Lincoln Child Center, including Chris, Joel, Kim, Aisha, Gwen, Kevin, Dee Dee, Ebony, Amber, Azita, Angelia, G, Jamie, Ivonne, Suzanne, Diosa, Brandon, Dawn, Amanda, Anthony, Ayesha, Dana, Imelda, Alicia, Marie, Matthew Williams, Christopher, Jason, Corey, Valarie, Summer, Crystal, Carolyn, Gina, Michelle, Christian, Abigail Gregor, Maitreya Rosiles and others. Thank you for being an incredible blessing in my life. Your R.A.M. enhanced friendships over the past year has taught me how to become a more caring clinician while maintaining a sense of humor.

To my niece, Jocelynn Evans, thank you for always making improvements to your personal and academic life. You always continue to strive for and achieve the best out of life.

To my daughter Rosie, thank you for being the most fantastic daughter on the face of the earth. You exemplify R.A.M. through your afro-centric teaching, counseling and mentoring. Colette and I will always love you because of the way you prayed for our relationship.

To my sister Sandra Berger (aka Sandy) and momma Mimi, thank you for your support and critical consciousness-raising dialogues. Sandy, thank you for being the best sister-in-law ever. You trusted me from day one with loving your best friend and roommate Colette and I will always love you for your non-judgmental trust in me.

To my sister Tesha Bonner-Flowers and her family, thank you for your love and support to my beloved. You and your family truly demonstrate R.A.M. to the fullest. You and my beloved have been going strong for 25 years, here is to another 25.

To my sister Martine Hall and her family, you are a powerful force in my beloved's life. I appreciate and love hearing about your friendship and witnessing your commitment to my beloved. It is moving to know that the course of your journey together has been over 25 years. Look forward to what is to come.

To my sister, Rachel A. Williams. Thank you for your steadfast prayer for and over the relationship that my beloved and I have. You have my beloved's back and we will always have yours.

To Demetra and Reggie Mack and the family, thank you for always praying for and over me and Colette. You embody R.A.M. in your everyday life as parents, community activists and leaders within the Oakland Community.

To my Joanna Fox and family, thank you for always supporting my professional accomplishments. I am so grateful for our relationship. Thank you for sharing your life stories and encouraging me over the past five years as friends. Your consistent R.A.M. friendship has benefited me enormously.

To my dear friend and colleague Victor Travis and family. Thank you for continual friendship and support. I appreciate your spiritual R.A.M. relationship, especially your ability to always show up and be present.

To my editor, colleague and dear friend Dr. Ben Baab and family, thank you for your authentic friendship and your continual commitment to edit my books with excellence. Thank you for always modeling R.A.M. as a colleague and friend.

To my editor's son, Will Baab, thank you again for configuring my magnificent book cover! You are the best!

To my fellow Airborne Rangers at the 1/75th Ranger Regiment in Savannah, Georgia and to my 173rd Airborne Paratroopers in Vicenza, Italy thank you for allowing me to experience my third rites of passage as a Black man. I will never forget the R.A.M.-intense training I experienced with both of these elite Army Infantry forces. This experience helped to solidify the R.A.M. resilient Black male that I am today. Thank you for your service to our country!

Most significant, I must thank my FedEx Kinkos family members at both the Richmond District and Sloat locations. Thank all of you including, Sabrina and Stefan. Sabrina, your assistance and encouragement over the past 10 years has been unforgettable.

To Uncle Barney and Auntie Elizabeth, thank you for always welcoming me and my family into your home. You both have amazingly joyful and welcoming Aloha spirits that resonate throughout the entire Big Island. I love you both dearly!

To one of my dear friends, Mr. Joseph Szlamnik (aka Big Joe) and son (Justin). Big Joe, thank you for being one of the most authentic friends I have ever had over a lifetime. Our monthly candid discussions have made my life easier to manage and navigate as one of the few Black males in the field of counseling.

To Dr. Brad Washington and family, thank you for always lending your ear to my concerns as a Black professional. Brad, your commitment to underserved migrant families, especially those with limited English skills, has set a precedence for educators around the world to model. Thank you for being a role model of academic excellence!

To my first rite of passage experience and alma mater, City College of San Francisco Ram football. Thank you for allowing me to grow as a young Black male on your squad. The coaches and staff inspired me to endure when life gets hard! Go Rams!

To all of my professors, counselors and administrative staff at my Alma mater, San Francisco State University. Thank you for mentoring me as a undergraduate and graduate student. Your encouragement and support, especially the Educational Opportunity Program (EOP) had a significant impact on my growth as an undergraduate and graduate student. Thank you for all of the educational services, teaching and counseling you provided me throughout the many years as a SFSU Gator!

And finally, to anyone whom I may have forgotten, thank you for all of your support and encouragement.

AARON L. HORN

Dr. Aaron L. Horn is a teacher, counselor and coach. Aaron was born and raised as a young child in San Francisco's Bayview-Hunters Point neighborhood. Although he moved away from Bayview as a young child, he has claimed Bayview because of his family of origin and love for his community. Dr. Horn began his career as an educator in the 1990's as a Program Coordinator for a non-profit agency called San Francisco Educational Services, previously located in the Bayview. As a young educator, he enjoyed establishing relationships with students and teachers from various cultures. While working in the community of Bayview, Dr. Horn attended San Francisco State University and completed his Bachelor's in Sociology and Master's in Education. It was at this point in Dr. Horn's career where he began his life-long passion for counseling underserved families.

During his work in the Bay Area, Dr. Horn worked as a counselor in group homes and in West Contra Costa Unified and San Francisco Unified School Districts. Subsequently, Dr. Horn served as a US Army paratrooper in various locations including Bosnia, Italy, Germany, and Egypt. After returning home from the military, Dr. Horn continued his work as an educator and counselor. In 2008, Dr. Horn received his doctorate degree in International Multicultural Education from the University of San Francisco. His research involved investigating the impact of caring relationships on young African American males' education. Shortly after his dissertation was completed, Dr. Horn published his dissertation into a book entitled *The Role of Father-Like Care in the Education of Young Black Males*. His research eloquently presents the lives of underserved families and how they endure a number of socio-cultural problems such as poverty, institutional racism, and community violence.

Afterwards, Dr. Horn continued his research and community work, focusing on poverty and inequity for underserved families as an educator. He later published an article on the language of the Yoruba people, a Niger-Congo tongue. He used this research to train Bay Area teachers in language acquisition and fluency in Black Vernacular English and its implications for teaching and learning. After working as an educator, Dr. Horn realized that his teaching was becoming more therapeutic. By this means, the families that Dr. Horn was working with began to engage in candid discussions regarding their mental health issues. As a result of these discussions, Dr. Horn decided to re-enroll at the University of San Francisco and pursue his life-long passion of becoming a therapist. During his tenure as a counseling psychology student, Dr. Horn co-founded the USF Marriage and Family Therapy Students of Color Support Group. In summer 2012, Dr. Horn received his Master's Degree in Counseling Psychology.

After graduating again from USF, Dr. Horn continued researching the impact of poverty and inequity on the lifespan development of young Black males. While working as a counseling intern for the San Francisco Juvenile Justice Center (JJC), Dr. Horn helped to increase awareness and understanding about the excessive incarceration regarding adolescents of color, particularly young Black males. As a result of his passion to educate and counsel incarcerated youth, he created a therapeutic instrument that helped to guide his work with clients and has been used by other clinicians at the JJC. Dr. Horn's innovative instrument, a personal accountability tool, has made a significant impact on clients at the JJC. Most significantly, Dr. Horn's social justice framework with its provision of culturally grounded treatment plans has shown positive outcomes with these clients. After completing his clinical internship at the JJC and continual research on poverty, Dr. Horn published his second book titled *I Got'Cho Back! Improving relationships with young Black males.*

For over 20 years, Dr. Horn has devoted his passion to the enhancement of the Bayview-Hunters Point community. He has received numerous awards and accolades, including "Community Advocate Award" from San Francisco State University and the "Edward J. Griffin Award" from the University of San Francisco. Dr. Horn is currently an Adjunct Professor at the University of San Francisco, Counseling Psychology Department and the owner of Horn Development Consulting (HDC), a professional coaching organization located in San Francisco, California. For those interested in Dr. Horn's teaching, counseling and coaching, please visit http://aaronlhorn.com for more information.

Made in the USA
San Bernardino, CA
27 September 2015